Drake's Road Book of the Sheffield and Rotherham Railway; With a Visiter's Guide to the Towns of Sheffield and Rotherham

RAIO fratellò d'mare

DEDICATED, BY PERMISSION, TO THE CHAIRMAN AND DIRECTORS OF THE
SHEFFIELD AND ROTHERHAM RAILWAY COMPANY.

DRAKE'S

ROAD BOOK

OF THE

SHEFFIELD AND ROTHERHAM

RAILWAY:

WITH A VISITER'S GUIDE TO THE TOWNS OF
SHEFFIELD AND ROTHERHAM.

Illustrated by a Map and Engravings.

LONDON:

HAYWARD AND MOORE.

BIRMINGHAM: JAMES DRAKE, 52, NEW STREET.   SHEFFIELD: WILLIAM
SAXTON.   ROTHERHAM: J. HINCHLIFFE.

1840.

ENTERED AT STATIONERS' HALL.

BIRMINGHAM:
PRINTED BY JAMES DRAKE, 52, NEW-STREET.

Univ ⓡ

TO THE

CHAIRMAN AND DIRECTORS

OF THE

SHEFFIELD AND ROTHERHAM RAILWAY COMPANY,

𝔗𝔥𝔦𝔰 𝔙𝔬𝔩𝔲𝔪𝔢

IS,

BY PERMISSION, RESPECTFULLY INSCRIBED,

BY THE

AUTHOR AND PUBLISHER.

May 21st, 1840.

Univ   *ft* ®

STANZAS

ON THE OPENING OF THE

SHEFFIELD AND ROTHERHAM RAILWAY.

BY EBENEZER ELLIOTT.

———

THEY come! the shrieking steam ascends,
  Slow moves the banner'd train;
They rush! the tow'ring vapour bends;
  The kindled wave again
Screams over thousands, thronging all
To witness now the funeral
  Of law-created pain.

Behold it, Osgathorpe, (a) behold!
  Look down, and cry, All hail!
Skies! brighten into blue and gold,
  O'er all the living vale!
Pale, ling'ring foxglove! you, ye trees!
Thou, wood of Tinsley! tell the breeze,
  That Hell's dark cheek turns pale!

For Mind shall vanquish time and space,
  Bid east and west shake hands,
Bring over ocean face to face,
  Earth's ocean-sever'd strands;
And on his path of iron bear
Words, that shall wither in despair,
  The tyrants of all lands.

Eternal river! (b) roaring still,
  As roar'd thy foamy wave,
When first each wild rose-skirted rill
  Heard moorland echoes rave,—
Thou seest, amid thy meadows green,
The goodliest sight that earth hath seen,
  Since man made fire his slave.

Fire kindling man! how weak wast thou!
  Ere thou hadst conquer'd fire!
How like a worm, on Canklow's brow,
  Thou shrank'st from winter's ire!
Or heard'st the torrent-gathering night
Awake the wolf with thee to fight,
  Where these broad shades aspire!

(a) Osgathorpe, Canklow, Winco, and Tinsley, are hills and woods, portions of the scene.
(b) "The D..r.

But he whom cold and hunger ban,
  Whom law and ease belie,
Who vainly asks his fellow-man
  For leave to toil and die,
Is sadder, weaker, than wast thou,
When, naked here, on Winco's brow.
  Thou didst the wolf defy!

In vain thou mak'st the fire a slave,
  That works, and will not tire;
And burn'st the flame-destroying wave,
  And rid'st on harness'd fire;
In vain, if millions toil unfed,
And Crompton's children, begging bread,
  Wealth-hated, curse their sire.

Fire-kindling man! thy life-stream runs,
  Ev'n yet, through sighs and groans;
Too long thy Watts and Stephensons
  With brains have fatten'd drones!
O Genius! all too long, too oft,
At thee the souls of clay have scoff'd,
  And sold thy little ones!(c)

Sold them to misery's dungeon-gloom,
  To rapine's menial blow,
To beggary's brawl-fill'd lodging-room,
  Where famine curses wo;
Then to the pest-den's workhouse floor,
To which good Christians send the poor,
  By stages sure and slow.

But lo! the train! On! onward! still
  Loud shrieks the kindled wave;
And back fly hamlet, tree, and hill,
  White steam, and banners brave;
And thoughts on vapoury wings are hurl'd,
To shake old thrones, and change a world,
  And dig Abaddon's grave.

Eternal river! roaring now,
  As erst, in earliest years,
Ere grief began, with youthful brow,
  To live an age of tears;
Thou hear'st; beneath thy forests high,
A voice of power, that will not die,
  While man hath hopes and fears.

He, conquering fire, and time, and space,
  Bids east and west join hands,
Brings over ocean face to face,
  Earth's ocean-sever'd strands;
And on his iron rod will bear
Words that shall wither in despair,
  The tyrants of all lands.

(c) I do not believe that men of genius are less able than other men to gain
their living: but if they attempt more, they are more liable to failure; but if
they live where none are . . . d of the . . . . . f their . . . . . is it surprising that they do not thrive

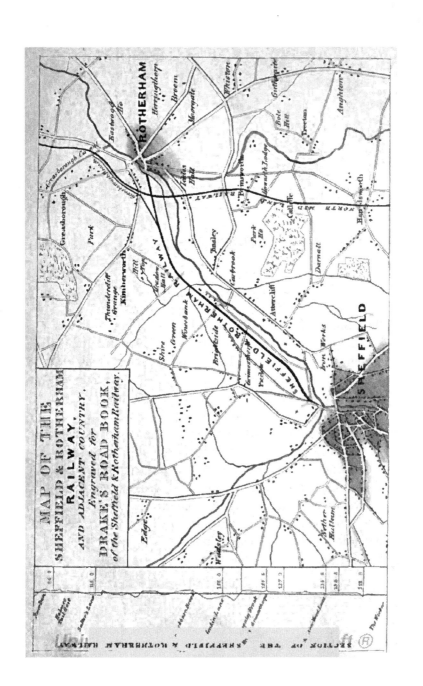

MAP OF THE
SHEFFIELD & ROTHERHAM
RAILWAY,
AND ADJACENT COUNTRY.
Engraved for
DRAKE'S ROAD BOOK,
of the Sheffield & Rotherham Railway.

ROAD BOOK

SHEFFIELD AND ROTHERHAM RAILWAY.

CHAPTER I.

HISTORICAL ACCOUNT.

THE Sheffield and Rotherham Railway is a monument of the public spirit and enterprise of its projectors of which they may well be proud. Severe was the contest which they had to maintain in the commencement of their great undertaking, and flourishing and honourable are the laurels which now rest on their brows. Could we add one floweret to that garland of honour, we should consider we had performed a worthy act. But our aim at present is higher than this. Our object in writing this volume is not to weave a wreath for the railway Company, but to carry out still further their praiseworthy designs. They have done all that Science and Art could teach them, to add lightning to the feet of the traveller. We would now humbly profess that we intend, by the aid of Minerva, Apollo, the muses, and all the deities that smile propitiously upon the wielders of the grey goose quill, to render his flight still more rapid. This we shall endeavour to do by cunningly beguiling each moment as it flies. Courteous traveller, we lay our volume at thy feet,—vouchsafe to make it the companion of thy journey. It will give to thy passage a quicker appearance; and, wherein is that less beneficial than making it actually more rapid? What would it avail thee were thy journey performed in as short a time as the head of Bagdad's monarch was immerged in the water-tub of the learned dervish, if that brief moment were crowded, as in his case, with the sorrows and toils of seven long dreary years?

Away, however, with this trifling, and to our task. Attend, then, in the first place, gentle reader, to the following brief Historical Account of the Sheffield and Rotherham railway,—its origination, its progress and completion, and its subsequent successful operation.

The project of constructing a railway between Sheffield and Rotherham was first brought before the public in the month of July, 1834. The principal design of its projectors appears to have been, to render coal cheaper at Sheffield ; and the saving upon which they calculated, was £30,000 per annum. The bill to invest the directors with the necessary powers, was first brought before parliament by lord Morpeth, on the 11th of March, 1835.

It was strongly opposed by the Duke of Norfolk, a few other landed proprietors, the Canal Company, and the River Don Company. One hundred and twenty highly respectable inhabitants of Rotherham also united with its opponents, and petitioned against it, on the ground that it would probably have the effect of causing the idle, drunken, and dissolute portion of the Sheffield community to flock to Rotherham. The railway Company, however, carried the day, being strenuously supported by the people of Sheffield, and also by the majority of the inhabitants of Rotherham. Upon the committee dividing on the preamble of the bill, two appeared against it, and twelve in its favour. On the 10th of June the committee reported the bill to the House; and on the 23rd it was read a third time and sent up to the Lords.

In the Upper House the Duke of Norfolk's influence proved more formidable; and on the 27th of July, the advocates of the bill had the mortification of beholding it thrown out in committee by a majority of 7 to 5.

Not at all daunted by the failure of their first attempt, the Company were soon in a condition again to take the field. On the 12th of February, 1836, their bill was a second time introduced into the House of Commons; on the 28th it passed through committee without a division; and on the 14th of April, having been read a third time in the lower House, it was again launched into the perilous seas where it had previously been stranded. Skilful was the piloting which was necessary in order to steer it into the now not distant haven. Twice it was read without opposition. On the 21st it went into committee. Here all the power of the opposition was brought to bear against it; and every nerve was strained by its advocates in order to bear it successfully through. Amongst other objections it was urged, that the deed executed by the shareholders in 1834 was invalid, owing to its not including the Greasborough branch,

for which this was the first time of making application.
This compelled the company to solicit time to prepare
a new deed; and with a little difficulty they obtained
a postponement of the question until May the 9th.
During this short interval, by means of great exertions,
the new deed was prepared and signed. At the appointed time the company were again before the committee ; and two days afterwards obtained a favourable
decision. Having been reported to the House of Lords
the bill was immediately read a third time; and on the
4th of July received the royal assent. Thus terminated
successfully the company's parliamentarian conflicts,
after having lasted from the 11th of March, 1835, to
the 4th of July, 1836.' By the act then obtained,
authority was given to raise a capital of £100,000, in
4,000 shares of £25. each, and £30,000 on mortgage.

The works were commenced in February, 1837, at
the Brightside cutting. From that time they proceeded rapidly without any impediment, or the occurrence of any incident calling for remark; and in the
month of October, 1838, were deemed in a sufficiently
perfect state to authorize the opening of the railway
to the public. This event took place on the 31st of
October, and was attended with all the pageantry, fes-
tivity, and excitement, which is usually manifested on
such occasions. Earl Fitzwilliam and a considerable
number of the neighbouring nobility and great landed
proprietors were present. So also were the Directors
of the North Midland railway, George and Robert
Stephenson, and many other illustrious individuals
interested in the success of this and similar schemes.
The order of the proceedings was as follows:—a trip

from Sheffield to Rotherham at twenty minutes
before eleven, which occupied seventeen minutes;
breakfast at Rotherham Court House; return trip to
Sheffield at twelve; and dinner at the Tontine Inn at
five.

The history of the railway subsequent to its opening
is happily marked by no tragical occurrences, by the
relation of which we might give interest to our narra-
tive. Monotonous as the strokes of the piston of a
steam engine, events have followed each other in re-
gularly recurring succession, and few days bear any
marks by which they can be distinguished from their
fellows. The opening of the Greasborough branch
took place on August the 10th, 1839. The following
is a brief summary of the traffic on the railway during
the first year of its operation. "The number of passengers carried (and that without the loss of life or
limb, or serious injury to any passenger) from November 1st, 1838, to October 31st, 1839, both days
inclusive, is as follows:—1838.—November, 37,876;
December, 44,614.—1839.—January, 28,071; February,
27,729; March, 30,034; April, 38,109; May, 50,325;
June, 37,500; July, 43,358; August, 39,882; September, 41,801; October, 36,076; making a total of
455,375." The amount of money received for these
passengers has been £13,204 16s. 3d. The shares at
present bear a premium of from £5. to £6.

So much for the past history of the Sheffield and
Rotherham railway. Were we disposed to indulge
ourselves in a prophecy of the future, very bright
would be the colours in which we should paint it; for
we cann t cl se our eyes t the vast incr as of traffic

which will flow upon this railway, when the sluices of the north and the south are opened into it by the completion of the North Midland line. However justly the inhabitants of Sheffield in general may complain of the distance at which the North Midland railway passes their town, the proprietors of the Sheffield and Rotherham railway, have good cause to congratulate themselves that it runs just where it does.

In the ensuing session of parliament the company intend to apply for an act to enable them to raise, at such times as they think fit, either by creating new shares or by mortgage, or in both those ways, any further sum they may require, not exceeding £70,000. The new shares will be offered in the first instance to the proprietors of original shares.

Before introducing our reader into the peculiar domains of the Fire-King and commencing our description of railway scenery, we shall, in accordance with the plan of our work, devote a chapter to the history and description of Sheffield.

CHAPTER II.

HISTORY AND DESCRIPTION OF SHEFFIELD.

THE town of Sheffield is situated upon the river Sheaf, near its confluence with the Don, and forms the chief town of the extensive Saxon Manor of Hallam, now called Hallamshire. It is a place of great antiquity, and derives its name from the river upon the banks of which it is situated. At the time of the Norman survey the manor of Sheffield was held by Roger de Busli, and the widowed countess of the Saxon Earl Waltheof, who had been beheaded for entering into a conspiracy against the Conquerer. It was subsequently possessed by the family of De Lovetot. It afterwards descended to the Earls of Shrewsbury, and from them finally passed into the possession of the Dukes of Norfolk. Edward I. granted various privileges to the lords of the manor; and they in turn released the inhabitants, in consideration of a fixed annual payment, from the feudal tenure by which they held their estates, and thus occasioned Sheffield to become a free town. Cardinal Wolsey after his arrest in 1530, was detained in the manor house for eighteen days, in the custody of the Earl of Shrewsbury. Mary Queen of Scots also during her fourteen years' captivity resided, with the exception of a few short intervals, in the same place or in the castle. During the civil war in the reign of Charles I., the inhabitants were in favour of the parliamentarians, and made a feeble effort to retain for them the town and castle. The Earl of Newcastle, however, with a party of royalists, quickly gained possession for the king, placed a garrison in the castle, and appointed Sir William Saville governor. The Earl of Manchester afterwards sent a force to attempt its reduction, and after a protracted siege, it was surrendered upon honourable terms, and soon afterwards by order of parliament demolished.

The town is pleasantly situated on a gentle eminence rising out of a spacious valley. It is sheltered on every side, except the north east, by a chain of lofty hills richly clothed with wood. It is nearly surrounded by the rivers Don, Sheaf, and Porter. Over the river Don a stone bridge of three arches was erected, in 1485, and was called the Lady Bridge, from a religious house dedicated to the Blessed Virgin, which stood near it. An iron bridge of three arches has since been constructed over the same river; and in 1828 an additional stone bridge of three arches was erected, for the purpose of affording an easier communication between the Rotherham and Barnsley roads, and the new corn and cattle markets. The bridge over the Sheaf consists of one arch, and was built in 1769, by Edward Duke of Norfolk. The town extends nearly a mile from north to south, and three quarters of a mile from east to west. The streets in the principal parts of the town have of late been greatly improved, both by the erection of new and handsome shops, and the substitution of modern and elegant fronts. The houses, which are chiefly of brick, and of a somewhat sombre appearance, are intermixed with many of very ancient character. The chief portion of the town is within the angle formed by the Sheaf and the Don, but there are considerable ranges of buildings on the opposite banks. Considerable improvements have taken place under the provisions of an act obtained in 1818, by which the town is well paved, and lighted with gas, from extensive works at Sheaf Bridge, and those of the New Gas Company, on Blonk Island. The town was formerly supplied with water from springs in the neighbouring hills, by means of private works on Crook's moor; but the supply becoming inadequate to the increasing demands of the town, a company with a capital of £100,000 was formed in 1829, and suitable works were erected.

The public subscription Library and Reading room occupies a commodious room in the Music Hall, and is supported by an annual subscription of one guinea from each of its members. A Literary and Philosophical Society was instituted in 1822. Its meetings are held in an elegant apartment of the Music Hall, which contains their apparatus, a collection of fossils, botanical specimens, and curiosities from the South Sea islands. There are three public news rooms; the oldest is in the East Parade, and is supported by an annual subscription of £1. 1s. each; another occupies a room in the music hall, and the third forms part of the handsome edifice, called the Commercial Buildings, which has recently been erected in High Street. The Mechanic's Library was established in 1824; it contains more than 2,000 volumes, and is open every evening. The Music Hall is a spacious and elegant building in the Grecian style of architecture. It is situated in Surrey Street, and was erected in 1824 ; it comprises on the ground floor a room for the public library, 38 feet long, and 35 feet wide; a reading room and saloon, and a spacious room for the Literary and Philosophical Society. The buildings also contain an elegant music room, 99 feet in length and 38 wide, with a well-arranged orchestra, and a handsome saloon, 35 feet long and 28 wide. The theatre and assembly rooms were erected in 1762, and form an extensive building of brick, handsomely ornamented with stone, and having a central portico supporting a pediment, The theatre is generally open from Oct. to Jan.

The Town's Trust has arisen from a grant made by one of the ancient family of Furnival, about the year 1300, and consists of property in lands and tenements, shares in the river Don navigation, &c., producing about £1,400 per annum, which is under the management of twelve trustees, resident in the town, elected by the freeholders, who have been lately incorporated, under the title of the " Town's Trust," or " Sheffield Free Tenants. " The income is applied to the maintenance of Lady's bridge, the keeping in order the pump in Barker pool, the repair of the church and the highways, the payment of three assistant clergy, and other charitable and public uses.

This town appears to have been distinguished at a very early period for the manufacture of articles of cutlery, for which the numerous mines of coal and ironstone in the neighbourhood rendered its situation peculiarly favourable. Chaucer, in his Canterbury Tales, mentions the "Sheffield Thwytel, or Whittel," a kind of knife worn by such as had not the privilege of wearing a sword, for the making of which, as well as the iron heads for arrows, Sheffield had, even then, become celebrated. Arrow heads, indeed, compose the arms or crest of the town. From that time the principal articles manufactured were implements of husbandry, including scythes, sickles, shears, and other sharp instruments of steel, till the middle of the last century, when considerable improvements were introduced, and great ingenuity displayed in the finer articles of cutlery. The superintendence of the trade was entrusted to twelve master cutlers, appointed at the court leet of the lord of the manor, with power to enforce the necessary regulations for its protection and improvement. In 1624 the cutlers were incorporated by an act of parliament entitled, "An act for the good order and government of the makers of knifes, scissors, shears, sickles, and other cutlery wares, in Hallamshire, in the county of York, and parts near adjoining;" and the government was invested in a master, two wardens, six searchers, and twenty-four assistants, consisting of freemen only, in number about 600. The master, who, with the other officers of the company, is chosen annually by the whole corporation, on retiring from office, nominates the senior warden as his successor; but if the latter be rejected by the company, he nominates another member, till one is approved of by the body: the wardens are chosen by the officers of the company from among the searchers for the time being. The master, wardens, and assistants, have power to make

by-laws for the regulation of the trade, and to inflict
penalties for the neglect of them ; and the jurisdiction
of the company, which is restricted exclusively to
affairs relating to the trade, extends throughout the
whole district of Hallamshire, and all places within six
miles of it. By an act obtained in 1814, permission is
given to all persons, whether sons of freemen or not,
and without their having served an apprenticeship, or
obtained from the company a mark for their goods, to
carry on business anywhere within the limits of Hallamshire. The privilege thus bestowed has been a
great means of advancing the trade to its present state of
perfection, by affording encouragement to men of
genius from every part of the country to settle in this
town ; and the competition thus produced has furnished
exquisite specimens of workmanship, in the finer
branches of the trade, which abound in the show-
rooms of the principal manufacturers, particularly in
those of Messrs. Rodgers and Sons, and excite the
admiration of the spectator. The cutlery trade em-
ploys from 8,000 to 10,000 persons. The principal
articles are table knives and forks ; pen and pocket
knives of every description ; scissors ; razors ; surgical,
mathematical, and optical instruments ; engineers' and
joiners' tools ; scythes, sickles, and files, of which
great quantities are manufactured and exported ; and
an endless variety of steel wares, which may be considered the staple trade of the town, though various
other branches of manufacture have been subsequently
introduced and carried to a high degree of perfection.

Connected in some degree with the cutlery, but
embracing a great variety of other objects, is the manu-

facture of ivory articles; but the principal branches of manufacture which have more recently been established, and in which the town has obtained a decided superiority, are spoons, tea and coffee pots, candlesticks, and a great variety of articles of Britannia metal, which are made in great quantities, and of every pattern; likewise silver-plated goods of every kind, among which are dessert knives and forks plated upon steel, tureens, épergnes, and services for the table, candelabras, ice pails, urns, and a variety of similar articles, of the most elegant patterns, and of the richest workmanship, which are generally known by the name of, "Sheffield plate with silver edges." The manufacture of silver plate in all its branches, from the most minute to the most massive articles, is also carried on to a considerable extent, and has obtained deserved celebrity. The most ingenious and highly finished specimens of cutlery displayed in the principal shops in the metropolis, and in those of the principal towns in England, notwithstanding their being stamped with the venders' names, are manufactured here; and so highly are the manufactures of this town esteemed, that they are found in every market in Europe, and exported in great quantities to every part of the globe. The making of buttons and button moulds, wire drawing, and the refining of silver, are also carried on; and along the banks of the rivers are numerous iron and steel works, in which the heavier castings are produced, and extensive works for slitting and preparing the iron and steel for the use of the manufacturers: among the manufactured iron goods are, boilers for steam engines, stove grates, of most elegant design and exquisite workmanship,) fenders, fire irons, and various smaller articles. There are also extensive factories for the weaving of carpets, and of horse-hair seating for chairs. In 1806, a type foundry was established with considerable success; and another was commenced in 1818, the proprietors having purchased the business of a house in London: both these establishments are now considerable, and supply type not only to printers in the provincial towns, but to several highly respectable houses in the metropolis.

The trade of the town has been greatly facilitated by its advantageous line of inland navigation. The river Don was, in 1751, made navigable to Tinsley, about three miles from the town; and, in 1815, a bill was obtained for enabling the proprietors of the Sheffield canal to connect the Don, at Tinsley, with the town, by means of a navigable cut, which was accomplished in 1819, thus forming a direct communication with the North Sea. Adjoining the basin of this canal, at the eastern extremity of the town, is a commodious wharf, where vessels can load and unload under cover; and also spacious warehouses and offices for the transaction of business. The basin is capable of containing more than forty vessels of about fifty tons' burden, many of which are constantly arriving from Hull, York, Gainsborough, Manchester, Leeds, Liverpool, and Thorn, at which last place vessels from London generally unload goods intended for Sheffield.

Sheffield's means of railway communication do not as yet extend beyond Rotherham; but the completion of the North Midland Railway, in the ensuing spring, will at once open to its inhabitants, in a range both of the southern railways, and of those which pass through the manufacturing districts of Yorkshire. We may, therefore, justly look forward to that period as a grand era from which to date Sheffield's accelerated increase in manufacturing celebrity and wealth; and though some of her more ardent well-wishers might have been desirous that so important a line should have passed nearer to her borders, yet none can refuse to admit the vastness of the advantages she will derive from the line which has actually been selected; and, we, especially, as retained at present by the Sheffield and Rotherham Railway, are bound to manifest exuberant joy that the whole of the railway traffic of Sheffield, both inward and outward, must necessarily pass along the rails of our fortunate little client. The opening of the Sheffield and Manchester Railway will, it is true, put an end to this boasting; but six or seven years, we are well assured, will elapse ere the power of steam manages here to twine together the rival roses of York and Lancaster.

The market was granted in 1296, to Thomas Lord Furnival; the market days are Tuesday and Saturday: the former, chiefly for corn, is held in the corn exchange; a handsome building, erected under an act of parliament obtained in 1827, by the Duke of Norfolk, on the site of the Shrewsbury hospital, which has been removed. The market for butcher's meat is held in a convenient situation near Newmarket-street; and adjoining to it is the market for eggs, poultry, and butter. The vegetable market, which consists of ranges of shops, is on the outside of the enclosure for the butcher's meat. The fruit market is held on the

south side of Newmarket-street; and the fish market,
which is well supplied with salt-water fish on Monday
and Thursday, and with fresh-water fish every day
during the season, at the back of the Corn Exchange.
The fairs for cattle and toys are on the Tuesday in
Trinity week, and on Nov. 28th. A cheese fair is also
held on the last-mentioned day, in which are sold many
hundred tons of cheese from the counties of Derby,
Stafford, Chester, and Lancaster.

, By the act of the 2nd of Wm. IV., cap. 45, Sheffield
has been constituted a borough, with the privilege of
sending two members to parliament. The number of
voters registered at the first general election under the
Reform Act was 3,508, of whom 3,056 polled. The town
is within the jurisdiction of the magistrates for the district, who meet in the town hall every Tuesday and
Friday, for the determination of petty causes; and the
Oct. sessions for the West Riding are also held here by
adjournment. A court is held every second week,
under the steward of the manor of Sheffield, for the
recovery of debts under £5; and a court of requests
every Thursday, for the recovery of debts not exceeding £5, of which the jurisdiction extends for several
miles round the parish. By the act of the 2nd and
3rd of William IV., cap. 64, Sheffield has been made
a polling-place for the West Riding. The Town Hall,
a spacious and commodious building, at the foot of the
hay market, was erected in 1808: It contains a large
and well-arranged room, in which the sessions are held;
and apartments for the use of the police magistrates,
the commissioners of the court of requests, and for
the transaction of public business. On the ground floor

is a prison for felons within the liberty of Hallamshire, with apartments for the keeper. The Cutlers' Hall, in Church-street, in which the business of that company is transacted, and their public meetings held, was erected in 1832. It is a neat and capacious stone building, ornamented with the arms of the company well sculptured; and contains, besides other offices, three large rooms in front for the transaction of business. On the second floor is a spacious dining room, elegantly fitted up, and ornamented with several well-executed portraits. In addition to an excise office and post office, there is also an assay office, erected in 1773, in order to relieve the manufacturers from sending their silver goods to London to receive the Hall mark.

The living is a vicarage, in the archdeaconry and diocese of York, valued in the king's books at £12. 15s. 2½d. The patron is the Duke of Norfolk; impropriators, P. Gell, Esq., and M. Lawson, Esq., late M.P. for Thirsk, who have alternately the right of presentation. Three stipendiary clergymen, who are independent of the vicar, and have an income of £250. each, are appointed to assist him by the church burgesses. These were incorporated by charter of Queen Mary, and hold certain lands and estates in trust, for the payment of the stipendiary assistants, and for the repairs of the church. They hold their meetings in a room over the vestry room of the church; and vacancies in their number are filled up by vote among themselves. The church, which is a spacious cruciform structure, with a central tower and spire, was erected in the reign of Hen. I.; but it has been so altered by repairs, that, with the exception of part of the tower and spire, and a few small portions of the interior, very little of its original character can be distinguished. The chancel contains the first production from the chisel of Chantrey, consisting of a mural tablet, with the bust of the Rev. James Wilkinson, late vicar, canopied with drapery, in Carora marble.   Many illustrious persons have been interred in this church, among whom were Mary, Countess of Northumberland; Elizabeth, Countess of Lennox, mother of the unfortunate Lady Arabella Stuart; Lady Elizabeth Butler; four of the Earls of Shrewsbury; and Peter Roflet, French secretary of Mary Queen of Scots. St. Paul's chapel was erected in 1720, by subscription, towards which Mr. R. Downes, silversmith, contributed £1,000: it is a handsome edifice, in the Grecian style of architecture, with a tower surmounted by a well-proportioned dome, and a cupola of cast iron; the interior is light, and elegantly ornamented, and contains a bust, by Chantrey, of the Rev. Alexander Mackenzie, with emblematical sculpture finely executed.   The living is a perpetual curacy; net income, £136; patron, the Vicar.   St. James's chapel, a neat structure, in the Grecian style of architecture, with a campanile turret, was erected by subscription in 1788: the interior is well arranged, and the east window is embellished with a beautiful painting of the Crucifixion, by Peckett.   The living is a perpetual curacy; net income, £160; patron, the Vicar; impropriator, Duke of Norfolk.   St. George's church, on an eminence at the western extremity of the town, erected in 1824, is a very handsome structure, in the later style of English architecture, with a lofty square embattled tower, crowned with pinnacles. The living is a perpetual curacy; net income, £365.; patron, the Vicar. St. Philip's church, near the infirmary, was erected in 1827, by grant from the parliamentary commissioners, at an expense of £13,970. 16s.; it is a neat edifice, in the later English style of architecture, with a square embattled tower, crowned with pinnacles. The living is a perpetual curacy; net income, £135.; patron, the Vicar; impropriator, Duke of Norfolk. St. Mary's church, in Brammall-lane, of which the first stone was laid by the Countess of Surrey, in 1826, is a handsome structure, in the later style of English architecture, with a tower and a porch of beautiful design; it was erected by grant from the parliamentary commissioners, at an expense of £13,946. 11s. 9d.; the site and the cemetery were given by his Grace the Duke of Norfolk. The living is a perpetual curacy; net income, £190.: patron, the Vicar. The Park church, dedicated to St. John the Evangelist, stands on three acres of land, given by the Duke of Norfolk, near the lofty summit of Park Hill. It is a Gothic structure, and will accommodate more than 1,000 persons. There are five places of worship for Independents, six for Wesleyan Methodists, and one each for Baptists, the Society of Friends, Unitarians, and Roman Catholics.

The free grammar school was founded by letters patent in the reign of James I., and endowed by Thomas Smith, of Crowland, in the county of Lincoln, with lands producing, in 1603, £30. per annum, which have been since exchanged for lands at Wadsley, producing, together with subsequent benefactions, a revenue of £175. 10s. The school is under the control of the vicar and twelve inhabitants of the town, who appoint the master, with a salary of £60. per annum: there are at present about twenty scholars on the foundation, who are gratuitously instructed in the classics. The present handsome school house, situated near St. George's church, was erected a few years ago, in lieu of the old structure in Town Head-street. The boys' charity school, at the north-east corner ·of the churchyard, was established in 1706; and the present school house, a neat and commodious edifice of stone, has been recently erected on the site of the original building: it has an income arising from a benefaction of £5,000 by Mr. Parkins, in 1766, aided by a donation from Mr. T. Hanby, which maintains six boys on the establishment, at an expense of upwards of £60. per annum, the past masters of the Cutlers' Company being his principal trustees: the whole revenue is about £284. per annum, with which, and annual subscriptions, eighty boys are maintained, clothed, educated, and apprenticed. At the opposite corner of the churchyard is a similar school, in which sixty girls are maintained, clothed, and educated, and afterwards placed out in service: a convenient school house was erected, in 1786, at an expense of £1,500. A school for reading, writing, and arithmetic, has also been established here, in pursuance of the will of Mr. William Birley, who, in 1715, bequeathed £900. in trust for the purchase of an estate, of the rental of which, one third was to be appropriated to the establishment of the school, one third towards the maintenance of indigent tradesmen, or their widows, and the remainder towards the support of a minister to officiate in the chapel of the hospital. The school of industry was established in 1795, and removed to its present situation in 1815: the buildings, which are upon an extensive scale, and well adapted to their use, were erected by subscription: there are 350 children in this establishment. A Lancasterian school for boys, established in 1809, and a similar institution for girls, established in 1815, are supported by subscription. National schools, in which 390 boys and 391 girls are instructed, are maintained in connexion with the National Society, which, in addition to a grant of £320. from the district society, has granted £650. towards the erection of the buildings; and a national school for 400 children has been erected at an estimated expense of £700, of which £350. was defrayed by the Lords of the Treasury, under an act passed in 1833. There are also numerous Sunday schools.

The Collegiate School is pleasantly situated in the vale of the Porter, and was opened in August, 1836. It belongs to a company of proprietors, and is conducted in conformity with the principles of the church of England. The Wesleyan Proprietary Grammar School, in Glossop-road, is a very large establishment. It has just been finished, and will accommodate 300 boys. The bestowment of a decidedly Wesleyan training was the principal object had in view by its projectors.

The Earl of Shrewsbury's hospital was projected by Gilbert Earl of Shrewsbury, in 1616, and completed, in 1673, in pursuance of his will, by the

Earl of Norfolk, Earl Marshal of England. It
is amply endowed for eighteen men and eighteen
women, who have each a comfortable dwelling; ten
shillings per week for each man, and eight shillings
for each woman, with an allowance of coal, coats,
and a gown annually. The original buildings were
recently taken down to make room for the new market
place, and the erection of the corn exchange; and a
neat range of buildings, in the later style of English
architecture, has been erected on the southern side of
the town, in the centre of which is a chapel. The
general infirmary was first opened for the reception of
patients in 1797, and, in a manufacturing town, where
so many artisans are continually exposed to accidents,
and their health materially injured by the processes of
many of the trades in which they are employed, has
been deservedly regarded as an object entitled to the
most liberal patronage and support. The premises,
occupying an extensive site about a mile to the north-
west of the town, and guarded against the too near
approach of other buildings by the purchase of thirty-
one acres of surrounding land, were erected by public
subscription, at an expense of nearly £20,000, including the purchase of the land. They are handsomely
built of stone, and form a conspicuous ornament in the
principal approaches to the town. In front of the
building is a neat portico, ornamented with statues of
Hope and Charity, finely sculptured; and the grounds
are enclosed by an iron palisade, with a central gateway, and a porter's lodge on each side. The internal
arrangements are extensive and complete, and the institution is supported by an income arising from dona-

tions and bequests, and by annual subscription.
Among the principal benefactions are, £200. by the
Rev. James Wilkinson, late vicar; £200. by Dr.
Browne, under whose auspices the establishment was
materially promoted; £1,000 by Mrs. Fell, of Newhall;
a donation of £2,000, and a subsequent legacy of £500,
by F. H. Sitwell, Esq.; and £6,337. 2s. 10d. bequeathed by the late Rev. Thomas Gisborne, who also
gave like sums to the infirmaries of Nottingham and
Derby.

The Botanical and Horticultural Gardens, which
were opened to the public in 1836, occupy about
eighteen acres of land in the picturesque valley of the
Porter.   The grand entrance is in Clarkhouse-lane,
and is a chaste Ionic structure, adapted to the model
of the temple on the banks of the Ilissus, at Athens.
The General Cemetery occupies an abrupt but broken
and verdant acclivity of Sharrow Vale, and extends
over upwards of five acres.   It was opened in July,
1836, and is one of the most beautiful establishments
of the kind in England.   The Cholera Monument is a
lofty, slender, and elegant obelisk. · It stands in the
Claywood cholera burial ground.   It was erected in
1834, in memory of those who had been swept away by
that terrific scourge.

The neighbourhood, which is rich in mines of iron
and coal, abounds also with quarries of excellent
stone, some of which, especially that at Grimsthorpe,
contain many admirable specimens of calamites; and
the coal shale and iron stone have beautiful impres-
sions of various vegetable productions.   In 1761, two
thin plates of copper were ploughed up on a piece of

land, called the Lawns, each containing an inscription commemorating the manumission of some Roman legionaries, and their enrolment as citizens of Rome. From the prevalence of iron ore, the waters of Sheffield have a slightly chalybeate property. The Rev. Dr. Robert Saunderson, Regius Professor of Divinity in the University of Oxford, and Bishop of Lincoln; and the Rev. Mr. Balguay, Prebendary of North Grantham in the Cathedral Church of Salisbury, and an eminent disputant in the Bangorian controversy, were natives of Sheffield: and Chantrey, the celebrated sculptor, was born at Norton, a village about three miles from it. Sheffield gives the title of Baron and Earl to the family of Holroyd.

CHAPTER III.

DESCRIPTION OF THE RAILWAY.

THE entrance to the Sheffield station is through a substantial and well-designed gateway facing up the Wicker, at the angle of the Barnsley new road and Saville-street. It is intended for passengers only; the entrance for goods being in Saville-street. On entering the station which is very commodious, a handsome and spacious shed, supported by cast-iron pillars, presents itself. It contains four lines of rails for the engines and carriages, and turn-rails at the end for reversing the position of the engines and carriages. The construction of the shed deserves notice, combining, as it does, strength with apparent lightness. A flagged pathway, raised a couple of feet above the level of the rails, renders the step into or from the carriages very easy and convenient. A similar shed is to be built in this station for the use of the North Midland Railway, with waiting room and offices suitable to the wants of the town of Sheffield; and passengers for Leeds or Derby and all intermediate places, will here take their seats, and proceed to their destination without any change of carriages.

Upon issuing forth from our entrenchments, we

behold, close to the line on the right, the works of
Mr. Brownell.   Saville-street and the river Don run
immediately behind these works, and from the opposite bank of the river rises the elegant and lofty
chimney of the New Gas Works.   The two conspicuous
chimneys which are a little more distant belong to the
new colliery, which has lately been established by the
Duke of Norfolk, and which is working the Yorkshire
Silkstone seam, at a depth of 126 yards.   A range of
lime-kilns, in which the lime is prepared by a process
altogether novel, are visible behind the colliery; and
the prospect is bounded by the verdant slope of Sheffield Park, in the midst of which St. John's church
is conspicuously situated.

Along the high ground on the left runs the new road
to Barnsley.   It gradually declines away from the
railway in the direction of the old road, with which it
forms a junction at Pitsmoor Bar.   The design of its
formation was to avoid the tremendous ascent of Pye
Bank, which all who have ever left Sheffield by the
north road will not fail to remember.

Were our traveller now to look behind him, and had
he power by some potent charm to dispel the murky
cloud that spreads itself over the landscape, he would
obtain a tolerable view of the town of Sheffield; and
would behold the tower of St. Paul's rising proudly
in the centre of the picture, and lifting its well-proportioned dome and elegant cast-iron cupola far above
all surrounding edifices.

The prospect speedily opens to a considerable extent
on the right.   As the eye ranges from the smoke-
capped buildings of Sheffield in the rear, to the beau-

tiful turrets of Attercliffe church in advance, it passes over a wide tract of country. Through this spacious valley winds the placid stream of the Don; but the eye cannot here catch a glimpse of its waters. The sight of this valley, and the park on its opposite acclivity, in which are the ruins of the Manor House, which formed the prison of the ill-fated Mary of Scotland, are well calculated to call up whatever remains of chivalric feeling that may exist in the bosom of the beholder. Perhaps he may apostrophise the meandering stream in some such elegiac strains as the following :—

> There, on Reflection's pensive breast,
> A shade of distant days will rest;
>   Where near yon ivied tower
> Thy stream would warble soft and low,
> Listening to sounds of royal woe,
>   Told to the midnight hour.
>
> On thee, with many a tear suffused,
> The beauteous captive nightly mused,
>   And in thy fleeting wave
> Saw the light bubble glittering rise,
> Then break in air,—" Behold," she cries,
>   " MARY, thy crown, thy grave ! "

Other associations of a less mournful character will also rush upon the mind whilst contemplating the valley which now lies before us. This is the famous " Valley of the Don," in which the author of Waverley has laid the scene of Ivanhoe, and with a description of which he opens that enchanting romance. " In that pleasant district," says he, " of merry England which is watered by the river Don,

there extended in ancient times a large forest, cover-
ing the greater part of the beautiful hills and valleys
which lie between Sheffield and the pleasant town of
Doncaster. The remains of this extensive wood are
still to be seen at the noble seats of Wentworth, of
Wharncliffe Park, and around Rotherham. Here
haunted of yore the fabulous dragon of Wantley;
here were fought many of the most desperate battles
during the civil wars of the Roses; and here also
flourished in ancient times those bands of gallant out-
laws, whose deeds have been rendered so popular in
English song." Such is Sir Walter Scott's description of the scene of our present excursion; and from
his account we perceive that the dragon-like monsters
that now sweep along it, are not the first creatures of
that species that have rendered it famous by their ex-
ploits. We cannot here resist the temptation of giving
our traveller a description, by the same hand, of a
landscape in this valley when it was covered by the
forest of Rotherwood, in order that he may compare it
with what meets his own eye as he dashes along it in
his steam-borne car. " Hundreds of broad short-
stemmed oaks, which had witnessed, perhaps, the stately
march of the Roman soldiery, flung their broad
gnarled arms over a thick carpet of the most delicious
green sward. In some places they were intermingled
with beeches, hollies, and copse-wood of various descriptions, so closely as totally to intercept the level
beams of the sinking sun; in others they receded from
each other, forming those long sweeping vistas, in the
intricacy of which the eye delights to lose itself,
while imagination considers them as the paths to yet

wilder scenes of sylvan solitude.   Here the red rays of
the sun shot a broken and discoloured light, that par-
tially hung upon the shattered boughs and mossy
trunks of the trees, and there they illuminated in
brilliant patches the portions of turf to which they
made their way." This looks like poetry, but it is
doubtless a correct representation of what often
greeted the eye of the Saxon swineherd, as he drove
his charge towards the castle of his Norman lord.   A
change, however, both great and surprising, has past
over this vision.   Forest, and castle, and serf too, have
vanished together ; or, if any remnant of Rotherwood
remains, it is but the unsubstantial shade of what
once bore the name ; and if every stone of the keep
and the turret has not been thrown down, only sufficient remain to attract the gaze of the antiquary, and
cause the artist to draw forth his pencil.   We would
fain pursue this theme ; but, whilst we mourned over
the loss of much of what was picturesque and romantic
in the England of eight centuries back, we would
pour our strains of loftiest panegyric on that spirit of
change, which, although it has stripped our land of her
beautiful forests, has also operated upon her inhabitants,—has torn the gorget from the neck of the
thrall, has dashed the bow from the grasp of the outlaw,
and the spear from the hand of the marauding knight.
To the reflections with which we have seen proper to
introduce our traveller into the valley of the Don it
behoves us now to put a stop: we must apply ourselves to our more legitimate task, of describing the
various objects which present themselves to his notice
as he sweeps along his iron pathway.

In the centre of the view we have been describing appear the Park furnaces, throwing forth copious volumes of fire and smoke, by which their position is even more distinctly revealed by night than by day. These furnaces are employed in reducing the argillaceous carbonates of iron, derived from Tinsley Common and other places adjacent. At present there is but one stack at work, which produces a larger quantity of metal than any other in Yorkshire or Lancashire, namely, twelve tons per day when the weather is favourable. The vitreous slag yields £500 or £1,000 per year for mending the roads. The process not only of smelting the ore and running the metal into pigs, but particularly of casting heavy articles, such as immense cylinders for conduit pipes, is very interesting, and may at any time be witnessed by the stranger. On the left the prospect is of course contracted, as we are proceeding along that side of the valley : Spittal Hill which is a little in the rear, and that of Hall Carr which is somewhat in advance, form the boundaries of vision in that direction.

At a distance of not quite half a mile from the station the line makes a curve to the left. It is not however of much consequence, as it has a radius of fully three quarters of a mile. On the right may now be seen, at a short distance, a white building called Royd's Mill, and a pile of brick buildings which constitute the silver refinery of Messrs. Reed and Co. The plantation very near to the line on the left is Hall Carr Wood.

In crossing Hall Carr lane on the level, the fires of the Manor Colliery are clearly distinguishable over the tops of the cottages on the right. Attercliffe church then forms the most interesting object in the right hand landscape, and of it we can obtain a very perfect view. This beautiful structure is in the early style of English architecture, and has an embattled tower crowned with pinnacles. It was erected in the year 1822, at a cost of £11,700, which was defrayed by a grant from the parliamentary commissioners. It is remarkable for the rich display of heraldic ornament which adorns its windows. The pulpit is surmounted with a curious and effective parabolic sounding board, which was invented by Mr. Blackburn the incumbent, and is described in the philosophical transactions for 1828. The living is a perpetual curacy, in the archdeaconry and diocese of York, of which the net income is £194. and the patron, the vicar of Sheffield. The old chapel can also be distinguished from the railway. It was allowed to fall into a sadly dilapidated state, but it has just undergone very considerable repairs.

The white house which occupies so elevated a position on the left is Woodhill house and was formerly the residence of Colonel Fenton, commandant of the Sheffield volunteers. Brightside lane runs on the right, between the railway and the river Don, and a little beyond it is Attercliffe Forge, an extensive pile of smoky brick buildings. Near the forge is New Hall, now in the occupation of Mr. Sanderson, the American merchant, who is master of the works at Attercliffe. New Hall was formerly the seat of Mrs. Fell, the liberal benefactress of the Sheffield Infirmary. The village of Attercliffe stands upon the turnpike road from

Sheffield to Rotherham, one mile from the former town. Its population is 3,741. The conspicuous windmill which also lies in the direction of Attercliffe Forge is the property of Mr. George Hill ; and near to it there was wont to be obtained an excellent species of cannel coal, with which the Sheffield Gas Works were for a considerable period supplied.

Upon arriving at a distance of a mile and a half from Sheffield, the range of hills, which has hitherto rendered our left hand prospect so very contracted, suddenly opens and discloses the village of Grimesthorpe. The appearance of this village from the railway, when first it bursts upon the sight, is exceedingly striking, and partakes in some degree of the grotesque. The most conspicuous object is the blackened brick building of the Grimesthorpe Grinding Wheel Company; the village lies beyond, and around it rise high hills, which have been invested with a somewhat romantic air by the extensive quarrying operations to which they have been subjected. The lofty hill in which the excavations appear, and whose bold brow is shaded with wood, is the classic Wincobank, of which Sheffield bards have often sung, and on which, say they,—

      " The golden cheek of eve rests loveliest."

But not only has Wincobank been the favourite resort of the poet and the admirer of Nature's exterior garb, but the mineralogist and the antiquarian may also be found wandering thither in search of the objects of their peculiar study. The one finds embedded in the brown sandstone the fossil remains of numerous plants which appear to have flourished beneath a tropical sun.   The other, ascending to the top of the hill and discovering amongst the bushes and thick underwood faint traces of castrametation, doubts not that he is standing within the sacred limits of a Roman camp ; and, as he looks down from his elevation, can almost see the burnished helmets of the legionaries winding through the valley, and glittering amongst the trees of the revivified forest.

The Grimesthorpe and Brightside road is crossed by an iron bridge with stone parapets. A culvert beneath the eastern wing affords a passage for the Baggaley Brook ; a small stream which, after washing the western foot of Wincobank, and turning the Grimesthorpe Grinding Wheel, crosses the line of the railway as it hastens to swell the waters of the Don. The village of Grimesthorpe does not continue in view for more than three quarters of a mile. On the right, however, a very interesting view is now disclosed. A somewhat lofty hill appears in advance, and upon its precipitous brow the village of Brightside stands, whilst the waters of the Don wend their sinuous course along its base. The prospect is very picturesque ; but it must be confessed that its beauty is in no degree enhanced by the dingy buildings of Brightside Forge, which, standing on the bank of the river, forms one of its most prominent features.

We now cross a private road by a beautiful stone bridge—one which is in fact the only ornamented bridge upon the line, and also the only one that is graced with parapets. The absence of parapet walls on this railway may be considered as one of its distinguishing features; and yet it is thought that it should

Uni   D   fi ®

have quite escaped the talented engineers of other lines, that were *le monstre*, in passing over a bridge, to feel at all inclined to make a digression to the right hand or the left, a wall would form but a very slight impediment to his wishes; and were he, on the other hand, rather inclined to preserve the even tenor of his way, still less would any beneficial purpose be answered by the two costly parapets. Perhaps, however, our friends in other parts of the kingdom may not exactly coincide with us in our ideas on this point, and may fancy that a few pounds sacrificed at the shrine of taste are well expended, whatever mere motives of economy might suggest. After crossing this bridge we have a still more interesting view of Brightside, which from our present position has a truly romantic appearance. By looking forward we can perceive that the hill on the brow of which it stands, has been divided in order to afford a passage for the railway; but before we enter this excavation we check our speed, and make a halt at the station which bears the name of the neighbouring village.

BRIGHTSIDE STATION.

The houses of Brightside stand chiefly on the right of the railway; but a few appear scattered on the left. The little wooden box which serves for a temporary station-house also stands on the left.

The pleasantness of its situation has caused Brightside to be much frequented by pleasure parties from Sheffield. On every fine Sabbath especially, the sallow artizan may be seen wending his way thither, to inhale the freshness of the country air, and enjoy the beautiful and extensive prospect which the hill affords. The opening of the railway has not been productive of much benefit to it in this respect. Those who, when performing their peregrinations on foot, were compelled to confine them within a circuit of a mile or two round Sheffield, can now ride to Rotherham for sixpence; and the consequence is, that the publicans of Brightside have the mortification of beholding their quondam customers gliding past their very doors to consign to the pockets of the more fortunate retailers of spirits in a more distant town, those gains which they had been accustomed to calculate upon as theirs. That the respectable inhabitants of Rotherham are satisfied with this state of things is more than we should like to assert. Some of them we know had much rather that the draff of the Sheffield pot-houses were emptied into any other place than their once quiet and moral town. Nay, some have ventured to malign even the railway company, and to charge them with breaking the laws of God in opening their railway on the Sabbath as a channel for this polluting stream to pass through. We would ask such objectors what they suppose the consequence would be were all the common sewers in Sheffield closed on the Sunday?

Immediately after leaving the Brightside station, we enter a deep cutting, made through the hill upon which the village stands. This excavation is about three quarters of a mile in length, and frequently forty feet deep. It is crossed by two bridges,—the first conveying the road to Wincobank, called Jenkin-lane, across the railway; and the second an occupation road, in a farm belonging to the trustees of the

Shrewsbury hospital, and occupied by Mr. Ellis. The stratification of the rock, which is here-beautifully developed, is what chiefly demands the attention of the traveller in passing through this cutting. The peculiar character of the geology of the valley of the Don has long caused it to attract the attention of scientific men. A paper was read on the subject at the Bristol meeting of the British Association, and it has frequently occupied the attention of the West Riding Geological and Polytechnic Society. Perhaps the following brief statement, as we cannot pretend to enter into detail, will enable the reader to understand the appearances which the sides of the cutting present:—At Ickles Hall, which is a mile and a half west from our present position, the Tinsley Park four feet ironstone lies at a depth of fifty yards below the Rotherham red rock. Twenty yards below the iron-stone, there is a thin seam of furnace coal; and sixty yards lower still, the High Hazles coal, which is four feet six inches thick. Ninety-one yards below this, there is a six feet seam; and seventy-eight yards below it, we find the Swallow Wood coal, which is six feet in thickness. After this follow the Park Gate seam, or Sheffield Manor coal, Walker's Furnace coal, and the Silkstone seam, which last lies about 440 yards below the Swallow Wood coal. Under the river all these beds lie horizontally, the one over the other, but just before they reach the line of the railway, they suddenly rise at an angle of about forty-five degrees, and all except the three last-mentioned reach the light. Of these strata the railway makes a partial section about the place where the

Swallow Wood coal bassets out. Were this section made at right angles to the strata, it is evident that it would present one uniform appearance from beginning to end; but as the angle which it makes with the line of inclination is somewhat less than a right angle, many strata are exposed to view as they successively rise to the surface. Beds of freestone, ironstone, (which may be distinguished by its rusty appearance,) and shale, interspersed with numerous little veins of coal, successively appear and disappear; but the Swallow Wood seam is the only coal measure of importance that is exposed to view. It is this seam which is at present worked at the pits of Messrs. Chambers, which we shall presently have to pass. What was obtained from the cutting was turned to profitable account by the contractor, who employed it in burning the ballast in which the sleepers are embedded. We must not however neglect to inform our traveller before we conduct him forth from this cutting, that it is in its right hand bank alone that the various strata are distinguishable; the great inclination at which they lie having rendered it necessary on the other side to shelve off the superior ones, to prevent them from sliding down upon the railway. Thus the one bank affords a pretty correct idea of the inclination of the strata, whilst the other exhibits their order with as much clearness as could be done by a coloured diagram. Towards the close of the cutting, the strata can be seen abruptly to terminate, what is technically termed a fault being made; and immediately afterwards the interesting appearance of their undulation is distinctly perceivable. But perhaps the reader may imagine that we are describing phenomena, which can be observed only by a pedestrian survey of the cutting. We can assure him however that the geological appearances we have described are so clearly marked, that notwithstanding the rapidity with which his steam car bears him along, a very little attention will enable him to notice them all.

Upon issuing forth from the cutting a wide prospect bursts in our view on the right, and a contracted but beautiful landscape is unfolded on the left. The one view embraces the wide valley of the Don, from Blackburn Forge, in the direction of Sheffield, to the Holmes Furnaces near Rotherham,—the glistering waters of the Sheffield canal and the tortuous stream of the Don occupying the centre, whilst Tinsley village and Park form the back ground, and the spire of Handsworth church rises above the distant trees. The lovely view in the opposite direction extends up the narrow but picturesque valley of the Blackburn Brook, and is beautifully bounded by the noble woods of Thundercliffe Grange. The Blackburn Brook rises in the neighbourhood of Chapel Town, and flowing by Meadow Hall, here unites its waters with those of the Don. The Grange, as it is elliptically called in the neighbourhood, is the seat of the Earl of Effingham. Keppel's column, a pillar raised in commemoration of that gallant admiral's honourable acquittal, can just be distinguished peering above the trees of the Grange.

The bridge, or rather the viaduct, over the Blackburn Brook, is composed of five beautiful stone arches. It crosses, in addition to the Brook, a private road and the head stream of Blackburn Park.

We now proceed through the Meadow Hall estate on an embankment twenty feet in height. The rails on this embankment are laid upon cross pieces of kyanized timber; whereas elsewhere the sleepers are of stone. Running along the side of Kimberworth Hill we make a curve to the right of three-quarters of a mile radius. After sweeping across two private bridges, and admiring for a moment the Don winding through the meadows on the right, we catch a glimpse of Jordan Dam, washing the very banks of the railway, just as all the external beauties of Nature are hidden from our view by the side of another excavation. Jordan Dam is an elbow of the Don, from which the river Don Company have recently made a new cut to Rotherham. This was done much to the annoyance of the railway company, whose bill was before parliament at the very time that the river company were empowered to make their alterations, and who were compelled thereby considerably and injuriously to divert their original line. The new cut is broad and deep enough for vessels of ninety tons burden, and is nearly two miles in length. It extends from Jordan Dam to the Holmes, and thence in a direct line to the vicinity of the Rotherham bridge.

The cutting into which we have now entered, is neither so deep nor so interesting as the former. The stratification of the rock presents a similar appearance, but is not quite as well defined. It will probably be observed that the strata here appear to incline in a different direction from those in the Brightside cutting. This, it would appear to us, must either be occasioned by a considerable undulation in the strata, as they rise from the valley, in a direction parallel with their line of inclination, or must be accounted for by supposing that the curve which we have made since we emerged from the last excavation has caused the railway to form with the ascending strata an obtuse instead of an acute angle.

The river Don company's new cut lies on the right, at a distance of only a few feet, but is concealed by the sides of the excavation. The smoke with which the air now becomes redolent, warns us of the proximity of the Holmes Furnaces; and, immediately upon emerging from the cutting, they burst upon our view, smoking, and flaming, and roaring, at but a few yards' distance on the right. This huge and unsightly temple of Vulcan assumes its sublimest appearance at night, when all surrounding objects are enveloped in darkness, and itself illuminated only by the fitful glare of the flame which it unceasingly throws forth. These immense iron works were founded by Samuel Walker, Esq., in the middle of the last century. This remarkable person, when twelve years of age, was an orphan, without money, and almost without education. In conjunction with his two brothers he established a small foundry; and, by his talents and industry, eventually rendered it one of the most flourishing in Europe. During the wars with America and France, immense quantities of cannon of the largest calibre were manufactured by him; and the iron bridges of Sunderland, Yarm, and Staines, and the Southwark bridge, at London, were cast at these foundries. Considerably less business is done here now than formerly; for, when Peace visited Europe in

1815, and, waving her olive branch, scattered plenty and prosperity over the nations, she frowned upon those who had forged the engines of war, smote down their proud looks, and ofttimes scattered their possessions. The Walkers then abandoned the greater part of their works, which have subsequently been divided, and let off to more humble speculators.

. On the opposite side of the line are the coal pits of Messrs. Chambers. From these the Holmes Furnaces are supplied ; and the brick bridge of one arch, which here crosses the railway, is for the conveyance of the coal and coke to the works.

More distant than the Holmes Furnaces on the right are Stubbs' Steel Works, and Habershon's Iron Works and Forge. Holmes Hall, the plain, square brick building, with a somewhat antiquated appearance, which presents its back to the railway at a very short distance, is at present a farm house, but was formerly the residence of the noble Earls of Effingham. Here we make our second and last halt.

HOLMES STATION.*

BEFORE carrying our traveller further on his way to Rotherham, we must make a short digression, as the Greasbrough branch, which we promised to describe, here diverges from the main line. As this branch, however, is mainly designed for the conveyance of coal from Earl Fitzwilliam's collieries at Greasbrough,

* We should anticipate at this station the speedy springing up of a large and populous town. We refer our reader to a prospectus, which he will find at page 9 of our advertising sheet, for the reasons on which we ground this opinion.

and of goods from the canal, and is seldom honoured
by the transit of passengers, it will not be necessary to
be very minute.

The branch to the Greasbrough canal, upon diverg-
ing from the main line, approaches Masbrough by a
curve to the northwards, and unites with the North
Midland Railway at Masbrough-street, near the foot of
the hill leading to Ferham, the residence of William
Swann, Esq. From this point, as far as the Greasbrough canal, the two railways run parallel with, and
close beside, each other.

A bridge carries both railways over the Masbrough
street. After which they encounter the high ground of
Masbrough Common, and pass under Back-lane, and
through a cutting nearly half a mile long and between
fifty and sixty feet deep, to the brook which separates
the township of Kimberworth and Greasbrough.
Here, on the left, appear Car House, now occupied
by Mr. Singleton, and The Clough, the residence of
George Wilton Chambers, Esq.; and, on the right,
the river Don, with Eastwood, beautifully situated on
the opposite hill, and Aldwark, amidst the thick and
picturesque woods in the distance. The railway now
passes over the Rotherham and Wentworth turnpike
road by a neat and substantial bridge; and through
the lowlands, called Greasbrough Ings, on an embankment from fifteen to twenty feet high, until it reaches
the Greasbrough canal. Here it terminates; and a
basin and wharf have been constructed for loading
and unloading goods from the canal,* which commu-

* From this wharf, in connexion with the Humber Union Steam
Packet Company, goods and merchandise can be shipped twice a

nicates with the river Don, at a distance of about 250
yards from this station. Uniting with the railroad at
this point, Earl Fitzwilliam has formed a branch railway to his collieries, which is traversable by the
locomotive engines and colliery waggons. On the
Greasbrough branch, only a single line of rails has
been laid down, as the conveyance of coal is the
almost exclusive purpose for which it is designed.

We now return to the main line. At the Holmes
station, the road from the Holmes to Masbrough,
which is called Salter's Lane, crosses the railway upon
its level. Upon leaving the station, we have the
village of Masbrough very adjacent to us on the left;
Rotherham church lifts its lofty spire in advance; and
the valleys of the Don and the Rother display their
beauties on the right. Masbrough, in addition to its
iron works, can boast of a pottery and a glass house;
and the Don is there crossed by a stone bridge of five
arches. The Rother rises in the county of Derby, a
little to the south of Chesterfield. After flowing past
that town, it waters, during the rest of its course, a
lovely vale renowned in song, and forms a confluence
with the Don near the town which we are fast ap-
proaching, and for which it has furnished the name of
*Rother*ham.

The North Midland Railway here crosses the Sheffield and Rotherham line by a magnificent viaduct.
The lofty embankment along which it proceeds can
be seen stretching up the valley of the Rother, almost

week, at the same rate of carriage as to Rotherham, and without
any charge of wharfage or cartage; and vessels discharging there,
can hay

as far as the eye can reach.   An imposing view is
afforded of a considerable portion of this vast work ;
when the eye has followed it as far as it can, the
mind still runs on, and views it penetrating the huge
mountains and spanning the enchanting valleys of
Derbyshire.   The desecration of this poetic valley by
the steam engine, has not been allowed to take place
unbewailed by the minstrels of the neighbourhood.
" Rother's Rose," sacred to poetry and sentiment,
shrinks from unfolding her red blossoms to the gaze of
every railway traveller, and blooms not beneath the
unpoetic cloud of vapour ; and the poet cares not to
have the eyes of a thousand travellers upon him as he
wanders through the once secluded glades of his be-
loved valley, nor yet to have his divine inspirations
mingled with the inharmonious din of a hundred iron
wheels.   The following elegiac strains would appear to
have been poured forth upon a farewell visit to this
beauteous, but now to the poet disfigured, vale :—

> How still and silent seems this valley now,
> Save when, at intervals, some rural sound
> Breaks on the listening ear.   How different far
> Will all things seem, when on the iron road
> The whirling steam car, with its waggon train,
> Shall shoot adown the vale : fire, vapour, smoke,
> Oft startling the lone wanderer, where e'en now
> The nightingale enchants the quiet shade.

We mourn not, however, the change ; and, were it
our's to possess the poet's laurel wreath, rather than
impede the progress of such works as this, we would
take the proud garland from our brow and cast it into
the flames of the locomotive itself.

The North Midland Railway strikes off from the Midland Counties Railway about a quarter of a mile from Derby.   It first runs up the Derwent valley, from which it emerges near Belper.   It then passes through the Amber valley, leaving Matlock six miles on the left.   It next enters the Rother valley and proceeds along it past Chesterfield and across the Yorkshire boundary as far as the Sheffield and Rother-ham Railway.   Proceeding northward, it passes three miles to the east of Barnsley, and two and a half to that of Wakefield.   Ten miles from Leeds it is joined by the Leeds and Manchester Railway, and shortly afterwards by the York and North Midland.   It ter-minates at the east side of Marsh-lane, at Leeds, and is there joined by the Leeds and Selby Railway.   Its total length is seventy-two miles; it passes through five tunnels in its course, and is expected to cost at least two millions sterling.   The summer of the present year will, in all probability, behold its com-pletion; and, at the same time, we shall have the happiness of again appearing before our readers as its historian, describer, and eulogist.

The view of Rotherham from this part of the rail-way, is beautiful and imposing; but as it lies directly in advance, it can only be seen by adventuring the head from the window of the carriage.   The church rises majestically on the left of the landscape; Can-klow Wood clothes the hills which stretch far away on the right; and, on the beautiful acclivity which forms the centre, rests a considerable portion of the fair town of Rotherham.   On the top of the hill the Methodist chapel stands conspicuously; and not far from it appears the New Poor House.   The mass of the town lies beyond the rising ground, and is consequently invisible.   Canklow Wood, which so beautifully overhangs the town, is the property of the Duke of Norfolk. On the summit of the hill which it envelopes, a little structure has been erected, on which the name of Boston Castle has been bestowed.   From this point the eye can range over a wide tract of country; and the prospect is as enchanting as it is extensive.

After crossing the headstream of the Holmes, we cross the river Don company's new cut by a handsome bridge of three arches, of which the centre one is iron and of thirty-six feet span.   Again we cross the headstream, and immediately afterwards the river Don, by a noble wooden bridge of seven arches. This bridge is well exhibited in the view of Rotherham, which forms the frontispiece of this volume.

Immediately after passing this bridge, we find ourselves beneath the spacious shed of the Rotherham station.   As this, however, closely resembles that at the other extremity of the line, a description of it is unnecessary.

We have now accompanied our traveller to the end of his locomotive flight.   By the potent agency of a little boiling water, he has been whirled from Sheffield to Rotherham.   We will now assume the more old-fashioned office of the mere topographer, and cause to pass before our reader whatever is most worthy of his notice in the famous and ancient town to which we have now conducted him.

CHAPTER IV.

ROTHERHAM.

THE town of Rotherham * is situated near the junction of the little river called the Rother with the Don. Baxter has given the true etymology of the name of this stream from the fulness of his Celtic knowledge, *Yr Odar*, (terminus,) the limit or boundary. There are three rivers of this name in England, and they are all limitary streams. A Roman origin has been claimed for Rotherham. About half a mile higher on the stream of the Don is a rectangular encampment, which has long been known by the name of Temple-borough, or Castle Garth by Templeborough. It is situated on the south bank of the river, a very small space being left between the outer agger and the water. The area is defended by a double agger, the outer line exceeding the inner considerably in height and thickness. The lines are parallel, and the space be-tween the two lines equal, except that it is much

---

* In introducing some few notices of the ancient history of Rotherham, we shall at once own ourselves indebted to Dr. Hunter's estimable work, "The History of the Deanery of Don-caster," and as this large and expensive work is necessarily in very few hands, we hope our readers will thank us for making more generally known this very small and condensed portion of its valuabl contents.

smaller on the side towards the north. The entrance
was on the south, where there was a depression in the
work exactly in the centre. A similar depression in
the north agger has at present the appearance of
having been no part of the original work, but made
since the whole plot was given up to the purposes of
husbandry. About 300 yards to the west of the camp
still higher on the river, is another earth work, but which
is probably only a fragment of some larger work, the
lines of which have been obliterated by the plough.

The form bespeaks it to be the work of a civilized
nation, and the Roman *Idicia* which are from time to
time discovered, leave no doubt that it was a work of
that people. Pieces of Roman brick-work and pottery
are found; and coins are also sometimes discovered,
of which the most remarkable is an Aureus of Vespa-
sian.

The industrious and generally cautious Horsley has
fixed upon Templeborough, as the site of the Morbium
of the Notitia. The work of Richard of Cirencester,
with its new Roman Itinerary, had not been produced
in the days of Horsley. In that Itinerary we meet
with a station called *Ad Fines*, lying between Chesterfield, as it is supposed, and Castleford, and this
station, till the appearance of that Itinerary unknown
to our antiquaries, has been placed near Templeborough, and the town of Rotherham is supposed to
have arisen out of it.

But there are no indications of anything resembling
a town in the immediate vicinity of Templeborough.
Rotherham, which is more than half a mile from the
camp, has no appearance of having been built on a

Roman model; and although the name of Rotherham may appear to be a reflection of *Ad Fines*, yet it is on the other hand to be considered, that if the Itinerary be not a genuine work, an admirable hint for the name of *Ad Fines* was afforded in the glossary of Baxter under the word Rotherham.

On the whole as the subject now stands, I would recommend to the good people of Rotherham, to be content with a Saxon antiquity, to which the early foundation of their church and the great extent of their parish justly entitle them.

LORDS OF ROTHERHAM.—In the times of the Confessor, Rotherham was held by Acun, as a manor of five caracutes. It was valued at £4, but at the time of the survey, the value through some cause has fallen to 40*s*. The new lord had one caracute in demesne and eight villains, and three borderers, who had two caracutes and a half; and there was a mill which however yielded no more than ten shillings rent. This, with the church, was Rotherham at the end of the eleventh century.

Acun was displaced with the other Saxon proprietors, and his manor was given to the Earl of Morton, who had subinfeuded Nigel Fossard before the date of Domesday. The family of Nigel granted Rotherham as a separate member of their fee, to a race of subinfeudatories. One of these was Eustace Fitz John, who received from Henry I., a declaratory or confirmatory charter of all his lands, in which are named those which he held of the fee of William Fossard. In conformity with this in the Testa of de Nevill, we find holding one knight's fee in Rotherham, of Peter de Mauley. The posterity of Eustace enjoyed a feudal superiority at Rotherham, till the town and church were given to the monks of Rufford. A branch of the family of de Vesci, bearing the hereditary name of Tilli, disputed with the posterity of Eustace the possession of Rotherham. Dodsworth, copying as it seems some ancient piece of evidence, says, " Robert de Tilli was the first conqueror or purchaser of Rotherham, and from him issued John de Tilli; and from John, Ralph Tilli, and the same Ralph forfeited and lost his lands of Rotherham, and King Henry, father of King Edward, entered into the same lands and held them as his escheat. John de Vesci in the reign of Edward I., gave all he possessed at Rotherham, to the monks of Rufford.

Dodsworth records that, in the answer which the abbot of Rufford returned to the commissioners under the *quo warranto* proceedings of Edward I., it being demanded by what right he claimed assize of bread and beer, tumbrel, pillory, standard of measure, of both length and weight, infangtheof, gallows,* and half the market;—he said he claimed in right of the moiety of the manor of Rotherham, which had belonged to Ralph de Tilli, &c.

---

* In conformity with this we find there is still a field known by the name of Gallow-tree-hill, on part of the common lands of Rotherham. Another kind of capital punishment was in use in Rotherham in the time of the middle ages, for among the many charges in the hundred rolls against Henry de Normanton, the under-sheriff, was one, that he had taken the horse, value forty shillings, of a certain thief hanged at Rotherham, &c.

For the next two centuries and a half Rotherham was under the peculiar patronage of the abbots and monks of the Cistertian house of Rufford, in Nottinghamshire. To that house the whole church belonged, and as they obtained an appropriation of it, it was served by a vicar as is now the case. All the feudal interests centred there. In the 13th year of Edward I., the abbot of Rufford obtained a grant of free warren in all his demesne lands of Rotherham.

Whatever the town of Rotherham might have been previously, it appears that after the Conquest it became something more than one of the agricultural towns of the district, for we find it had a market and fair while still in the hands of the Vescis. Of the origin of this privilege, which was much coveted, and doubtless very valuable in early times, we have no account. It appears to have been a prescriptive right, and may possibly have originated in the Saxon times, when the church of Rotherham was the only place of resort to a wide district, for the performance of the rites of Christianity; for many are the instances in which we find the meetings for traffic held at the places which were peculiarly sacred to the purposes of religion. Rotherham had unquestionably both a market and fair long before we have any reason to think that Sheffield enjoyed either of those privileges. King Edward I., in the 35th year of his reign, 1307, granted to the people of Rotherham another market, which was to be held on Friday, and a fair, yearly, at Midsummer. Two years after, another charter was granted for a market and fair at Rotherham, probably on the resumption of the former right or for what reason cannot be discovered, for the market is on the same day, Friday; the fair however is not at Midsummer, but on the eve, day, and morrow of St. Edmund, and the five following days. This grant was made to Edmund de Dacre; and Dodsworth notices one to the same effect, except that the market was to be on the Monday granted to the abbot of Rufford.

With these advantages, situated as it was upon one of the principal high roads of the kingdom, the communication between London and Carlisle, being in the line of Mansfield, Rotherham, and Wakefield, population would flow in upon Rotherham, and it would acquire more definitely the character indicated by the word *town* in the present use of it. The number of its chantries, the devotion of property to public uses, and the existence of streets possessing distinct appellations, all bespeak that Rotherham was, in the middle ages of our history, a place of some consideration, though its name does not appear in our chronicles; and having no residence of its lord, it affords in those periods very little matter for the topographical historian.

The name of Rotherham occurs but seldom in the history of the public affairs of the kingdom. The Queen of Scots rested a night there, in her journey from Bolton to Tutbury; and King Charles I., when a prisoner in the hands of the Scots, was brought from Wakefield to Rotherham, and after resting a night, (in the house in High Street, which is now the bank,) was carried to Mansfield.

The people of Rotherham zealously espoused the parliament cause; and the vicar, John Shaw, a most uncompromising partisan, escaped very narrowly when the town was taken by Lord Fairfax, by lying for three days and nights in the church steeple, while the Earl's forces were in possession of the town. His own published account of his escape, is of a marvellous and almost incredible description. It was on Rotherham Moor that the people assembled when the first act of hostility in this part of the kingdom was committed, the burning of the out-houses of Sir Edward Rodes, at Great Houghton. This was in September, 1642. The townspeople immediately proceeded to throw up works about Rotherham, and it was settled as a parliamentarian garrison by Lord Fairfax. We may perceive with what enthusiasm the people at large entered into the contest, when it is stated that even the school boys of Rotherham fought against the Earl with courage and pertinacity ; about thirty undertaking the management of a drake, which was planted at the entrance of the bridge, and did considerable execution against the assailants on the hill. The garrison fought till all the powder they had was expended, when they yielded the town on what Shaw the vicar calls honourable terms.

THE COLLEGE OF JESUS OF ROTHERHAM.—The splendid foundation of archbishop Rotherham, is at once the most prominent and by far the most interesting feature of its history. Thomas Scott, or as he was afterwards called, De Rotherham, was born on August 24th, 1423. He says of himself that he was born at Rotherham, and in that particular part of the town where afterwards he planted the college. He was baptized in the church of Rotherham, and lived there till he removed to King's College, Cambridge.

On the accession of Edward he was nominated one of
his chaplains, and as in those days civil and ecclesiastical offices were often united, he was made secretary
to the king, the keeper of the privy seal, and finally, in
1474, lord high chancellor.

His ecclesiastical preferments were not less splendid.
He was provost of Beverley and of Wingham; archdeacon of Canterbury; in 1467, bishop of Rochester;
1471, bishop of London; and finally, in 1488, made
archbishop of York. He died at Cawood, on May 29th,
1500, and was sumptuously interred in his own cathedral.

 On the feast of St. Gregory the Great, 1482, he laid
the foundation of an edifice at Rotherham, which was
designed for the foundation of a college; and on
January 12th, 1483, being then archbishop of York, by
his own ordinary metropolitical authority, he erected
one perpetual college, consisting of a provost and two
fellows; and inducted, by the delivery of a ring, the
provost and fellows into the possession of the building
he had erected. The description of the site of the college is, a piece of land lying between the river and the
Abbot's Close, called the Imp Yard. An imp yard is
what is now known by the term nursery garden. Le-
land visited Rotherham while still the college was
flourishing. He says, " Rotherham is a meately large
market town, and hath a large and faire collegiate
church. The college was instituted by one Scott,
archbishop of Yorke, otherwise caullid Rotherham,
even in the same place where now is a very faire college sumptuously builded of brike,* for a provost,

* Several small portions of the original beautiful brick work
still rem..... ....   Coll. ....

V prestes, a scholemaster in song, and VI chorestes;
a scholemaster in grammar, and another in writing.''
It is presumed to have been one of the first edifices in
this part of the kingdom built of that material, as it
became a popular saying in the neighbourhood, "As
red as Rotherham College." It lived through the
attacks which King Henry made upon the foundations
of our ancestors; but it fell never to rise again beneath
the act of the 1st year of Edward VI. for the suppres-
sion of charities, colleges, and guilds. Its possessions
were seized and granted out in parcels to different
persons, and the building itself much altered, but
still retaining some marks of its pristine character, has
at last become an inn.

THE CHURCH OF ROTHERHAM.—The church of
Rotherham is one of the most beautiful in the diocese;
it is in one instance called the church of St. Mary, but
is more commonly called the church of All Saints or
All Hallows. All Saints' day was the feast of dedica-
tion at Rotherham, and is still observed as the day on
which the *Statutes* are held.

It was erected in the reign of Edward IV., and archbishop Rotherham,* whose heraldic insignia of three
bucks trippant appears upon it, was, if not the sole

* In another place Dr. Hunter says: "The church of Rother
ham which appears to have been rebuilt by him from the foundation, is itself a fabric of surpassing beauty; and the vestments of
his priests, and the utensils for the altar, were of the most costly
fabric and the most gorgeous description. A catalogue of them is
given by the archbishop himself, and fully bears out this statement.
Chalices and cups, basons, crosses, of the richest description;
vestments of coloured velvet and cloth of gold, to the number of
more than a dozen, are mentioned. Other persons contributed to
give the church an appearance of uncommon splendour.

founder, yet a principal contributor to a work, which, without such assistance, was beyond the means of even so extensive a parish; aided by the funds of a wealthy monastic establishment. It is built of the red stone of the neighbourhood. It presents to us a complete model of the ecclesiastical architecture of England in what is perhaps its purest age ; more adorned than in the preceding century, but not with that extreme richness of minute ornament which appears in buildings of half a century later. We enter by a noble porch on the south side, to a lofty and spacious nave with side aisles. The transverse beams of the cross are of the same height with the highest part of the nave; and at the intersection rises a tall and graceful spire, with pinnacles rising from its base, and accompanying it to about a third of its height, and crockets to the top. The head of the cross is so constructed as to afford private recesses for the chantries * which were founded in the church, and opportunities for processions to the high altar, by having two chapels, one on each side in the angle made by the cross beams with the head of the cross.

The chapels are of the same height with the sides within, and the clerestory windows of the nave have others correspondent to them, through which light is admitted to the chancel.

The old font, perhaps a relic of the Saxon church, is in the churchyard. There are three stalls on the

* The valor of King Henry mentions five chantries in the church, viz., the chantry of the Holy Cross, St. Mary, Our Lady, St. Catherine, and the chantry of Henry Carnebull, who was archdeacon of York, and one of the executors of archbishop Rotherhap

south side of the altar, and a slanting niche may be observed, cut through the substance of a very thick wall, through which a view was admitted of what passed at the altar to persons assembled in the south chancel. The north limit of the transverse beam is separated from the rest of the church by some beautiful cancella. Here, as it seems, was the chantry of Henry Carnebull; and the large altar tomb against the north wall, with an enriched arch over it, may have been his monument. The church within is well pewed and lighted with gas, and proper regard is paid to its being kept in good order. The Rev. Thomas Blackley, is the vicar; the Rev. Frederick Blackley, curate; and the Rev. Mr. Hugile, evening lecturer.

PUBLIC INSTITUTIONS. — THE GRAMMAR SCHOOL was founded, as it is said, by Lawrence Woodnett, Esq., of Lincoln's Inn, and Anthony Collins, Esq., of London, who, by deed dated September 1st, 1584, conveyed to certain trustees, lands (supposed to be crown lands) at Rotherham, Masbrough, and Brinsworth, together with a building called the town hall, for the purpose of establishing a grammar school; but it seems that as early as the 3rd of Elizabeth, 1561, the sum of £10. 15s. 4d. was paid to the masters employed in a grammar school out of the profits of the country; most probably a reserve made on the dissolution of the college.

Robert Saunderson, the divine and antiquary, was educated at this school; and perhaps reflects more honour on this institution than any other name connected with it. He was born at Sheffield, and removed with his father to Gildwith in his early childhood,

Charles Hoole, a kinsman of Bishop Saunderson, and one of the most celebrated schoolmasters of his day, was one of the masters of this school. The Rev. Benjamin Birkett was for some years master to this school, and, since his death, after a lapse of some time, the Rev. Joshua Nalson, A.M., has been appointed.

The scholars have a claim to a fellowship and two scholarships in Emanuel College, Cambridge, founded by John Freston, of Altofts, in turn with other schools, when they are not claimed by the scholars of the school of Normanton. There is also a claim on a fellowship of Lincoln College, Oxford. This school forms part of a building which was erected in 1829, on the site of the old town hall, by public subscription, amounting to near £2,000, and which comprises the library, the newsroom, and the dispensary. This latter excellent institution has been nobly sustained, and perhaps is nowhere much more needed, than in a district where the labouring class are, from the nature of their employment, subjected to many accidents and injuries. This institution, since its establishment in 1806, to the present time, 1839, has afforded surgical aid and medicine to 15,800 afflicted poor persons. Mr. J. Goodall is the resident apothecary and secretary.

THE LIBRARY contains upwards of 3,000 volumes of books; and we dare venture to say, that a more judicious and valuable selection will be seldom found. Miss Turner is the librarian.

Opposite to this building is the Court House, a large and handsome fabric, built at an expense of upwards of £5,000, with a noble court room, in which is held the quarter sessions, public meetings, &c.; and other spacious rooms, well adapted for the transaction of the great weight of business which, as the centre of the wapentake of Upper Strafforth and Tickhill, has to be disposed of here.

HOLLIS's SCHOOL was founded by Thomas Hollis, who lived at Rotherham, and was buried there in 1663. He was a nonconformist, and placed the patronage of this school in the hands of the minister of the dissenting congregation which was formed there; he was the principal contributor to the erection of the Unitarian chapel, with which this school is connected, and which was built in 1705. Of this chapel the Rev Jacob Brettel, author of "The Country Minister," a poem too little known, and other poems and elegant translations, is the minister.

THE FEOFFEES' SCHOOL, in the Crofts, was built in 1776. The yearly income of this school is stated to be about £100.; of which, £50. is paid to the master, and the residue expended in providing clothing and books for twenty-eight boys and twenty girls, who are instructed in reading, writing, and arithmetic. Great attention is now paid by the gentlemen who form the present feoffees, to the interest of the children attending this school. Mr. John Mycock is the master, and Mrs Mycock the mistress.

THE BRITISH SCHOOL was built by subscription in 1833, in which education on the Lancasterian system is given to children of such of the labouring class as choose to avail themselves of this means, on payment of a small weekly sum. The schools will accommodate 200 of each sex. Mr. Sharp is the master of the boys' school, and Miss Eliza Turner mistress of the girls' school.

THE INDEPENDENT CHAPEL, at Masbrough, was built principally at the expense of Samuel Walker, Esq., and has, within the last two years, been considerably enlarged, and the interior received much tasteful and elegant improvement; which, together with the advantage of being warmed in winter, by a new apparatus, renders it a most comfortable and pleasant place of worship. With this chapel is connected the Independent college, erected in 1795, for the education of ministers of the Independent connexion: it has since been enlarged, and is capable of accommodating twenty-five students, who are instructed in classics, mathematics, rhetoric, and composition, and attend regular lectures on theology. Dr. Williams was the first president and theological tutor, who was succeeded by Dr. Bennett, now of London, and afterwards the Rev. Clement Perrot. The Rev. W. H. Stowell is now the theological tutor, and highly respected minister of the chapel; and the Rev. Thomas Smith, A.M., the classical tutor. Some of the most acceptable and talented amongst the ministers of the present time, of this denomination, received their education here.

THE METHODIST CHAPEL, in Talbot-lane, built in 1805, and since twice enlarged, is a handsome and spacious structure, capable of holding upwards of 1,500 hearers, and is worthy of the highly respectable, influential, and increasing, denomination to which it belongs; and whose exertions at Rotherham, as at other places, have been crowned with great success.

The present ministers are the Revs. William Leech, James Bromley, and W. H. Taylor. With this, as indeed with every other place of worship at Rotherham, large Sunday schools are connected.

THE METHODIST NEW CONNEXION have a chapel in Westgate, but no regular minister appointed.

THE BAPTIST CHAPEL, at the bottom of Westgate, built in 1836, is a small but very elegant structure, in the Grecian style, and is at once an accommodation and an ornament to this end of the town. The Rev. James Buck is minister.

Great alterations and improvements have been made in Rotherham within the last twenty years. The streets, which are in many places being widened, are well paved, flagged, and lighted with gas; almost every house in the town is supplied with excellent water; the low and old buildings which deformed the High-street and other parts of the town, have, in many instances, given place to good substantial erections, with handsome fronts; and it may be reasonably supposed that very few years will find still further and more important improvements and additions effected, called for by and calculated to meet the increased business which the railways must necessarily bring into the town. One striking and considerable improvement we must not omit to mention, namely, the widening of the top of Westgate; for which purpose from £2,000 to £3,000 was subscribed, and which will now present a spacious entrance, formed of lofty and handsome buildings, of which, the Ship Hotel forms the first and most distinguished object, supplying, as it does, a striking contrast

building which lately presented itself under that
name.

The corn and cattle markets, always considerable,
have been rapidly increasing in importance, particularly
the latter : within the last twelve months, about double
the amount of business was transacted to what was
done the previous year. In addition to the numbers of
Manchester butchers who have long frequented this
market for the purchase of fat cattle, many purchasers
from Leeds have lately been present; and, when the
North Midland opens its increased facility of inter-
course and conveyance, no doubt corresponding increase in numbers may be calculated upon, from this
and other places on the line. Perhaps very few
places out of London can at times furnish a finer show
of cattle than Rotherham market.

CHAPTER V.

VICINITY OF ROTHERHAM.

Leaving the town eastwardly, on the right of the road leading to Doncaster is Clifton, the elegant mansion of Henry Walker, Esq.; and a little further on, and on the left of the road, Eastwood House, built by the late Joseph Walker, Esq., and now the residence of James Sothern, Esq. Two miles from Rotherham is Aldwark Hall, " embosomed in woods, among which the river Don meanders until it retires into, and is lost amongst, the thick foliage of Thrybergh Park," where, three miles from Rotherham, beautifully situated, rises Thrybergh Hall, a handsome Gothic structure, erected by its present possessor, Colonel Fullerton. About one mile to the right of the road from hence, is Ravenfield Hall, the family mansion of the Bosviles, now the residence of Thomas Walker, Esq.

Between six and seven miles from Rotherham, the traveller comes to the pleasant and picturesque village of Conisbrough, where the majestic keep of the demolished castle arrests the eye; and where, higher up in the village, the ancient tower of " the church the hill top crowns " Sir Walter Scott, in a note to Ivanhoe, says, " There are few more beautiful or striking scenes

in England than are presented by the vicinity of this
ancient Saxon fortress.   The soft and gentle river Don
sweeps through an amphitheatre in which cultivation
is richly blended with woodland; and on a mount
ascending from the river, well defended by walls and
ditches, rises this ancient edifice, which, as its name
implies, was, previous to the Conquest, a royal residence of the kings of England." A barrow in the
vicinity of the castle is pointed out as the tomb of the
memorable Hengist; and various monuments of great
antiquity and curiosity are shown in the neighbouring
churchyard.

Southwardly of the town, on the road leading to
Worksop, Mansfield, &c., the hand of improvement
has been busy, as the elegant residences of South
Terrace and South Grove manifest; further on, on the
left of the road, is Moorgate, formerly the residence of
Samuel Tooker, Esq.; and which, with its beautiful
grounds, plantations, &c., then formed the most attractive feature the neighbourhood could exhibit: it
is now a boarding school.   Further on, Boston Castle,
a shooting box built by Thomas Earl of Effingham,
crowns the summit of an eminence, which affords one
of the most splendid bursts of varied and striking
scenery which this part of the country, rich as it is in
such views, has to show.   A little further on is the
residence of John Oxley, Esq.   On the lower road,
southwardly of the town, is the Broom, the residence
of John Boomer, Esq., from whence the road diverges
to the left, through Wickerley, famous for its quarries,
whence Sheffield is supplied with grinding stones, past
Bramley to the charming village of Maltby; from

whence a foot road leads amongst the quiet of a beautifully secluded dell, through which the winding rivulet
"wanders at its own sweet will" to Roach Abbey;
and few, indeed, are the lovely spots on this green
earth which display a richer diversification of se-
questered sylvan beauty, hallowed by its venerable
vestiges of monastic grandeur,—relics of the olden
time,—than does this attractive spot,—

> "Where the graceful ivy greenly creeps
> O'er the grace of hoar antiquity."

, We return to the town, and pursue the outlet by
Bridgegate. Passing over the bridge, on the centre
of which stands what was formerly a chapel, but is now
the gaol, and over the canal bridge, we come to Masbrough; a part of the suburbs which sprung up during
the rise and prosperity of the iron trade carried on there
by Messrs. Walker. Masbrough has to boast being
the birth-place of one of our best and most original
modern sons of song, Ebenezer Elliott; who, best
known by his least distinction of the " Corn Law
Rhymer," has poured forth his thoughts in fervid, mu-
sical, and glowing strains, which will live while poetry
can touch the heart, and when the debatable question,
now too much mixed up with his verse, shall have
become one of the " things which were." Passing
through Kimberworth, the road turns abruptly to the
right, and about four miles from Rotherham is the
entrance to Thundercliffe Grange, the seat of the Earl of
Effingham; and a little further, on the right of the road,
amidst a wood of magnificent oaks, rises a lofty Doric
pillar, built by the Marquis of Rockingham, in honour

of Admiral Keppel; from hence the road continues to
Chapel Town, Wharncliffe, Wortley, Peniston, &c.
Another road, after passing over the bridge, takes a
sudden turn to the right, and about one mile from
Rotherham, leads to the steel works belonging to
Messrs. William Oxley and Co. The extensive works
of the Birmingham Tin Plate Company, and the New
Park Gate Colliery, belonging to Earl Fitzwilliam,
from which, by an extension of the Sheffield and Rotherham Railway, as shown on the map, coals are
conveyed to Sheffield. A little further on, the road
passes through Rawmarsh to the Rockingham Works,
celebrated for the splendid specimens of china manufactured there by Messrs. Brameld. One of these, a
dessert service, made for his late Majesty, consisting
of upwards of 200 pieces, excited general admiration
from the beauty of the material, the excellence of the
workmanship, and elegance of taste displayed in its
production. They have lately introduced a novel
article in china bedsteads, which is stated to be under
the immediate patronage of her present Majesty. A
visit to these show rooms will highly gratify the curious
in porcelain; the best white glaze being considered the
clearest and most perfect white that can be imagined.
Little more than a mile further is the considerable
village of Wath. Here, in his youth, with a shopkeeper
of the name of Hunt, lived the author of " The World
before the Flood;" * and here too, the idol of his early
worship, she who formed the " starlight of his boy-
hood," immortalised in his exquisite poem of " Han-
nah," resided.

* James Montgomery, Esq

Returning to where this road branches off at Mas-brough, another road, passing Masbrough brewery, Messrs. Singleton and Wingfield, the Phœnix foundry, belonging to Mr. Sandford, the glasshouses of Messrs. Close and Clark, and the Effingham works, belonging to Mr. James Yates, in whose show rooms the visiter will find great variety of beautiful specimens of iron and brass castings in stoves, fenders, &c., and in iron-stone china letters for signs and ornaments for deco-rating buildings, of which new and beautiful articles Mr. Yates is the sole manufacturer and patentee. The road passes Carr House, late the residence of William Fenton, Esq., and now of John Singleton, Esq.; and about one mile from Rotherham is Barbot Hall, the residence of Lord Howard. Of this place a beautiful writer says : * " The site of this pleasant mansion commands a magnificent semicircle of many miles extent. The town, the River Don, Moorgate, Broom, Clifton, Eastwood, Aldwark, and the woods of Raven-field and Thrybergh, are all included in the prospect."

The village of Greasbrough is about a mile fur-ther, and another mile the entrance to Wentworth Park, a visit to which will afford the lover of magni-ficent scenery a high gratification. The splendid palace-like mansion, the woods, glades, lawn, and waters; are all grand and striking, and, connected and harmonised, as they now are, by judicious planting, form a magnificent whole, while the cloud-capt height of Keppel's column, the pyramidal elevation of Hoober Stand, and the mausoleum, with its " classic dome,"

* Rhodes's Excursions in Yorkshire, &c.

and interior with " richest sculpture graced," give to different points of view a beauty and grandeur rarely surpassed.

The west end of the town has been the scene of most striking and considerable additions and improvements. Here an elegant chapel has lately been built by the Baptists; here is the Rotherham corn-mill, the property of Mr. James Hodgson; the extensive brewery of Robert Bentley, Esq., who has just erected a malt house on such a scale as to form a considerable architectural ornament to this entrance. Above this rises the New Union Poor-house, built at an expense of upwards of £8,000; presenting, from the mass of building of which it is composed and the elevation on which it stands, a most imposing appearance. A little beyond, on the brow of the hill, forming part of Moorgate plantations, is pointed out as the site of a new cemetery; a company for the promotion of which desirable object is now forming, with every probability of succeeding in their undertaking.

Viewed from this wooded eminence, the viaduct, forming part of the North Midland Railway, which crosses the road to Sheffield, forms a fine feature in the scene. It consists of twenty-five arches, including two of seventy-two feet each span over the old river, and is, indeed, a noble specimen of massive architecture, which reflects upon Mr. Buxton, the contractor, the highest and most unquestionable credit.

APPENDIX.

SHEFFIELD AND ROTHERHAM RAILWAY.

OFFICERS.

DIRECTORS.

William Vickers, Esq., *Chairman.*

Mr. John Booth, *Deputy Chairman.*

William Ibbotson, Edward Vickers, William Jackson, Thomas Linley, William Swann, John Spencer, Samuel Jackson, James Roberts, E. I. Heseltine, G W. Chambers, William Glossop, J G. Clark, George Knowles.

Solicitors.—Mr. Thomas Badger and Mr. Henry Vickers. (The transfer registration books are kept at Mr. Vicker's office, Sheffield)

Engineer.—Mr. Frederick Swanwick.

Secretary.—Mr. Thomas Pearson.

Superintendent and Resident Engineer.—Mr. Isaac Dodds.

DEPARTURE OF TRAINS.

FROM SHEFFIELD,

At $7\frac{1}{2}$, $8\frac{1}{2}$, $9\frac{1}{2}$, $10\frac{1}{2}$, $11\frac{1}{2}$, $12\frac{1}{2}$, a.m.; and $1\frac{1}{2}$, $2\frac{1}{2}$, $3\frac{1}{2}$, $4\frac{1}{2}$, $5\frac{1}{2}$, $6\frac{1}{2}$, $7\frac{1}{2}$, $8\frac{1}{2}$, p.m.

FROM ROTHERHAM,

Every hour from 8 a.m., until 9 p.m.

SUNDAYS, FROM SHEFFIELD,

At 9 and 10 a.m.; and at $1\frac{1}{2}$, $2\frac{1}{2}$, $4\frac{1}{2}$, $5\frac{1}{2}$, $6\frac{1}{2}$, $7\frac{1}{2}$, $8\frac{1}{2}$, p.m.

FROM ROTHERHAM,

At $9\frac{1}{2}$ a m., and at 1, 2, 3, 5, 6, 7, 8, 9, p.m.

The Station Gates will be closed precisely at the times above specified for the departure of the Trains.

Parcels for Rotherham may be booked, free of charge, at Messrs. Fisher and Holmes, Nursery and Seedsmen, Market Place, Sheffield

An Omnibus runs on the arrival of each Train, (fare 4d.,) passing the Tontine, Albion, Commercial, King's Head, and George Hotels; and through the heart of the town, up the Glossop Road, as far as the first toll bar, within a few minutes' walk of the beautiful Botanical Gardens, the Cemetery, the Collegiate and Wesleyan Proprietary Schools, and some of the finest views in the neighbourhood. The Omnibus returns by the same route, to the Sheffield Station, in time for each train to Rotherham.

NORTH MIDLAND RAILWAY.

ARRIVAL AND DEPARTURE OF THE TRAINS.

BETWEEN DERBY AND SHEFFIELD.

Departure from Sheffield.	Arrival at Derby.
5 30 a.m.	7 45 a.m.
9 15 „	11 30 „
12 0 noon.	2 15 p m.
2 0 p.m.	4 15 „
6 0 „	8 10 „

SUNDAY TRAINS.

6 30 a.m.	9 0 a.m.
9 30 „	12 0 noon.
6 0 p.m.	8 25 p.m.

Departure from Derby.	Arrival at Sheffield.
5 55 a.m.	8 0 a.m.
9 15 „	11 30 „
12 45 p.m.	3 0 p.m.
3 15 „	5 30 „
8 0 „	10 15 „

SUNDAY TRAINS.

9 0 a.m.	11 30 a.m
3 0 p.m.	5 30 p.m.
5 40 „	

Uni

BETWEEN LONDON AND SHEFFIELD.

Departure from London.	Arrival at Derby.	Arrival at Sheffield.
6 0 a.m.	12 30 p.m.	3 0 p.m.
9 0 „	3 15 „	5 45 „
1 0 p.m.	7 45 „	10 15 „
8 30 „	5 40 a.m.	8 0 a.m.

SUNDAY TRAINS.

8 0 a.m.	3 0 p.m.	5 30 p.m.
8 30 p.m.	5 40 a.m.	8 0 a.m.

Departure from Sheffield.	Departure from Derby.	Arr. at London.
5 30 a.m.	8 0 a m.	3 30 p.m.
9 15 „	11 45 „	6 30 „
12 0 noon.	2 30 p.m.	9 30 „
2 0 p.m.	4 30 „	11 30 „
6 0 „	8 25 „	5 30 a.m.

SUNDAY TRAINS.

9 30 a.m.	12 0 noon.	7 30 p.m.
6 0 p.m	8 25 p.m.	5 30 a.m.

BETWEEN BIRMINGHAM AND SHEFFIELD.

Departure from Sheffield.	Departure from Derby.	Arr. at Birm.
5 30 a.m.	8 0 a.m.	10 15 a.m.
9 15 „	11 45 „	1 45 p.m.
12 0 noon.	2 30 p.m.	4 33 „
2 0 p.m.	4 30 „	6 30 „
6 0 „	8 25 „	10 45 „

SUNDAY TRAINS.

6 30 a.m.	9 0 a.m.	11 15 a.m.
9 30 „	12 0 noon.	2 0 p.m.
6 0 p.m.	8 25 p.m.	10 45 „

Departure from Birming.	Arrival at Derby.	Arrival at Sheffield.
3 15 a.m.	5 40 a.m.	8 0 a.m.
6 45 „	9 0 „	11 30 „
10 30 „	12 30 p.m.	3 0 p.m.
1 0 p.m.	3 0 „	5 30 „
5 30 „	7 45 „	10 15 „

F 4

SUNDAY TRAINS.

3 15 a.m.	5 40 a.m.	8 0 a.m.
6 45 ,,	9 0 ,,	11 30 ,,
12 45 p.m.	3 0 p.m.	5 30 p.m.

NOTE.—Passengers may be booked through between LONDON and SHEFFIELD, and BIRMINGHAM and SHEFFIELD, by the above Trains, at the respective Railway Stations at those places. Trains run between DERBY, NOTTINGHAM, LOUGHBROUGH, and LEICESTER; and Coaches to and from LEEDS, YORK, &c., (those to and from York, in conjunction with the trains of the York and North Midland Railway). Places by Coaches, in connexion with the North Midland Railway, may be bespoken at the Branch Railway Office, in Euston Square.

A Quarter of an Hour is allowed at Derby for Refreshment.

ROTHERHAM.

MAGISTRATES, PUBLIC OFFICERS, &c.

Colonel Fullerton, Thrybergh Park; Henry Walker, Esq., Clifton; The Rev. George Chandler, Treeton; T. B. Bosville, Esq., Comsbro; Thomas Walker, Esq., Ravenfield Park; and Lord Howard, Barbot Hall, Magistrates and Commissioners of Assessed Taxes.

Rev. John Lowe, Swinton; John Aldred, Esq., Rotherham; Commissioners of Assessed Taxes.

Mr. John Oxley, Clerk to the Magistrates, and Commissioners of Assessed Taxes for the Upper Division of Strafforth and Tickill.

Thomas Badger, Esq., Coroner for the County of York.
Mr John Bland, High Constable, and Inspector of Weights and Measures for the Upper Division of Strafforth and Tickhill.

UNION POOR HOUSE.

Mr. Worsley, Governor; Mrs. Worsley, Matron; Rev. J. Hugill, Chaplain; Mr. Joseph H. Turner, Surgeon; Mr. John Barras, and Mr. R. T. Barras, Relieving Officers; John Oxley, Esq., Clerk and Superintendent Registrar to the Union; W. F. Hoyle, Esq., Auditor.

FEOFFEES OF THE COMMON LANDS. (1840.)

The Feoffees of the Common Lands of Rotherham, are twelve in number, elected by the freeholders and rate payers. Their income amounts to about £600 a year, which is distributed in charities, doles, coals, &c., &c., to the poor inhabitants, and to the improvement of the town; there are at present two vacancies to be supplied. The following gentlemen, with the earl of Effingham, at present constitute this corporate body, viz.,—

Messrs. Benjamin Badger, Greave; Thomas Badger, Thomas Bagshaw, Edward Pagdin, Sen., Henry Walker, C. Nightingale, John Nightingale, William Earnshaw, Robert Bentley.

An Act for a Local Court for the recovery of debts, of not more than £15, was obtained on the 29th of July, 1839. F. Maude, Esq., is appointed Judge, and E. Newman, and W. F. Hoyle, Esqrs., Clerks.

POST OFFICE.

Post Mistress, Mrs Wilson.

Delivery of Letters. — London Letters, 12½ noon. — Hull ditto, 1 p.m. — North ditto, 3 p.m.

COACHES, &c.

FROM THE STATION.

The Times— From Doncaster for the nine o'clock Train, returns to Doncaster after the arrival of the three o'clock Train, except on Sunday, when it leaves on the arrival of the ten o'clock Train.

The Commander in Chief—From Doncaster to meet the one o'clock Train, returns to Doncaster on the arrival of the six o'clock Train from Sheffield.

The Retford Coach— From the Crown Inn, Retford, on Monday, at 5½ a.m.; Tuesdays and Thursdays, at 8 a.m., and Saturday at 4 p.m.—From the Railway Station, Sheffield, on Sunday at 9 a.m., and Monday, Wednesday, and Friday, at 3 p.m., in time for Coaches to Gainsbro', Tuxford, Newark, London, and all parts of the South, and in summer time will run daily. The above Coach will pass through Wickersley, Bramley, Maltby, Sunk Island, Oldcoates, Blyth, and Barnby Moor.

The Pelham. — From the Crown Inn, at $\frac{1}{4}$5 a.m., through Wickersley, Maltby, Tickhill, to Bawtry, Gainsbrough, Louth, Lincoln, &c., and returns at 8 p.m.

The Packet Coaches — From the Crown Inn, at 6 a.m , to Thorne water side, through Conisbrough, and Doncaster.

The Transit — From the Crown Inn, at 8 a.m. to York, through Doncaster, returns at 8 p.m.

The Eclipse — To Doncaster, at 10 a.m., and returns at 4 p.m..

The Louth Mail — Through Wickersley, Maltby, Tickhill, Bawtry, Gainsbrough, to Louth, at $9\frac{1}{2}$ a.m., and returns at 3 p.m.

The London Mail — To Doncaster, at $\frac{1}{4}$12 a.m., and returns at $\frac{1}{4}$1 p.m.

WATER CONVEYANCE.

River Dun Company's Wharf — Vessels every day to Thorne and Hull, &c.

Pearson and Co. — Vessels in connexion with sailing Brigs, to Stanton's Wharf, London, and with the Victoria, Gazelle, and Yorkshireman Steam Packets. Agent, John Copeland, Esq.

Hull, Humber, and Steam Packet Company — Boats from the Bridge, or *Fleck's Wharf,* on Wednesdays and Saturdays, to their Wharf, 1, Humber Place, Hull, in connexion with the Wilberforce, Vivid, and Water Witch Steam Packets to London. William Fleck and Co., Agents.

Thomas Smith — Vessels to Manchester, Lancashire, &c., every fortnight.

Thomas Wright — Doncaster Market Vessels with Corn, &c., to Sheffield.

John Newbold — New Park Gate, Gainsbrough Canal Vessels.

CLARK'S

METALLIC HOTHOUSE MANUFACTORY,

55, LIONEL STREET, BIRMINGHAM.

The above Establishment has been placed by its Proprietor under the sole management of Mr. John Jones, whom that able Horticulturist, London, pronounces to be, in his judgment, "decidedly the best Hothouse Builder in Britain," and whose elegant structures have long formed the chief points of attraction in the extensive Botanic Gardens, both of Manchester and Birmingham. The great and flattering encouragement which Mr. Clark has received from the principal Nobility and Gentry of the United Kingdom, during the last twenty years, and more especially since entering into the engagement with Mr. Jones, above referred to, affords the most convincing proof of the vast superiority of his Metallic Hothouses and Conservatories over all others; and the spontaneous testimonials to the same effect, which have emanated from various quarters in which they have been introduced, all tend to establish and confirm the fact. Mr. Clark is also well known as the Manufacturer of Copper Sashes of the most exquisite workmanship, and which are adapted, not only for the mansions of the opulent but for churches, and all other public buildings; they have likewise been extensively introduced into the splendid plate-glass windows of the first-rate shops in London, and other large towns; for which, indeed, their extreme lightness, combined with great strength and durability, render them peculiarly eligible.

COALBROOK-DALE CHINA.

PATRONISED BY THE SOCIETY OF ARTS,

JOSEPH JOHNSON'S GLASS AND CHINA ROOMS,

61, AND 63, FARGATE, SHEFFIELD.

J. JOHNSON

Begs most respectfully to announce to the Nobility, Gentry, and the Public in general, that having enlarged and newly fitted up his extensive Rooms, he has added to his stock of Glass, China, and Earthenware, a splendid assortment of the celebrated COALBROOK-DALE CHINA; the Manufacturers of which have had presented to them, by the Society of Arts, their *Gold Medal* for its superiority.

J. J.'s arrangement with this company will enable him to offer to his Friends the newest and best patterns in China, Dinner, Dessert, Tea and Breakfast Services, &c., manufactured in the Kingdom.

Complete Services, with Armorial Bearings, Crests, Initials, &c., painted upon each piece; and Glass made and cut to order on the shortest notice,

The favour of a call will be highly esteemed.

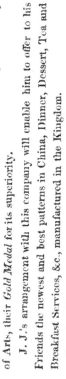

Palmer's Metallic Wick Candles and Lamps.

A 2

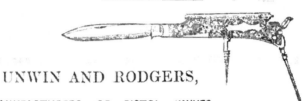

UNWIN AND RODGERS,

MANUFACTURERS OF PISTOL KNIVES,

FINE

PEN, POCKET, DESK, FRUIT, AND SCISSOR
KNIVES,

LOCK, SNECK. DAGGER, DIRK,

AMERICAN, INDIAN HUNTING,

AND

SELF DEFENCE KNIVES,
LANCETS,

IMPROVED PEN MACHINES, &c. &c.

No, 23, BURGESS STREET, SHEFFIELD.

JOHN SKINNER,

Sheffield,

MANUFACTURER OF

SCISSORS, KNIFE SHARPENERS, PLUMBERS' SHAVEHOOKS,

AND

STEEL PENS.

THESE Pens are so universally used and approved as to
render comment unnecessary. It will be sufficient to say, for the
information of those who have not tried them, that they are made
from Steel of a particularly elastic quality and exquisite temper,
and subjected to a process which effectually prevents their being
corroded by the ink; and so perfect is the principle upon which
they are constructed, that one trial will be sufficient to prove their
superior utility.

Sold by all Dealers in Steel Pens.

HOLMES ESTATE,
SITE OF ROTHERHAM NEW TOWN.

The owner of this extensive and valuable estate has instructed Mr. William Flockton, Architect, to lay out some of the best parts, in Convenient Lots for Building Purposes. It is a circumstance of rare occurrence that an opportunity for investing Capital to such advantage presents itself. The vast increase in the Value of Property in particular Districts, consequent on those magnificent Works, the Railways, in no place exceeds, if it equals, the advantages obtained in the immediate neighbourhood of Rotherham, but more especially on the Holmes Estate. The Grand Line of Communication from the North to the South of Great Britain by the North Midland Railway. The Sheffield and Rotherham Railway joining hand in hand the two Towns; and the New Canal of the River Don; all these pass in different directions through the Estate, giving an almost Unparalleled Facility of Communication from the very threshold of Manufactories erected here, with all parts of this realm, and the whole World. Few persons will doubt but that along the line of the North Midland Railway, and at the Junction of the Sheffield and Rotherham Railway and Canal, with the North Midland, a new Town will of necessity spring up. Here will be the Stations and Warehouses of the two Railways and Canal; and it is not improbable that the celebrated Cattle Market of Rotherham will be removed to adjoin the Railways. As a Situation for Manufactories, it stands without a rival. The Neighbouring Lands abound with Minerals of the first Quality; there is an exhaustless supply of excellent water for Steam Power,—an article frequently of more value for that purpose than the Land itself. It is the prevailing opinion that the heavier branches of the Sheffield Trade will be gradually removed into this Neighbourhood; and of this there can be no doubt, when the immense advantages to be obtained are so apparent. Distance from Sheffield, and insufficient roads, might have been fairly urged against this opinion before the Railway was established; but now there is the best of roads, and the distance is annihilated. A Merchant may leave his Villa on the West of Sheffield, and be at his Works near Rotherham in little more than fifteen minutes. Lots of Land to suit the convenience of persons will be laid out along the line of, and having a frontage, to the Canal and Railways.

The price will be such as to induce persons to embark their Capital on this eligible Site, and also those who have no immediate intention of building to take plots prospectively. It is impossible to state the price in an advertisement, as it will, of course, vary with the situation.

Plans of the estate may be seen, and further particulars had, at the offices of

MR. W. FLOCKTON, ARCHITECT,
DEVONSHIRE STREET, SHEFFIELD.

W. FLECK AND COMPANY,

IRON AND LEAD MERCHANTS,

CHEMISTS, &c.,

WHOLESALE AND RETAIL,

BRIDGE WHARF, ROTHERHAM.

DEALERS IN

Block Tin, Tinned Plates, Bar and Rod Iron;

SHEET, PLATE, AND HOOP IRON;

STEEL OF ALL KINDS; GLASS BOTTLES;

PATENT SHOT;

RED AND WHITE LEAD; SHEET LEAD AND LEAD PIPES;

Paints, Oils, and Colours;

VARNISHES, DRUGS, AND DRYSALTERY GOODS;

WHARFINGER'S COMMISSION

AND

GENERAL SHIPPING AGENTS.

CROWN INN

POSTING ESTABLISHMENT

AND

GENERAL COACH OFFICE,

ROTHERHAM.

J. SHAW

BEGS leave most respectfully to return thanks to the Nobility and Gentry for the patronage and support with which he has hitherto been honoured; and further begs leave to assure them, that no exertion on his part shall be spared to merit a continuance thereof.

COMMERCIAL GENTLEMEN and others may depend upon that sedulous attention being paid to their comfort, which, with the superior accommodation this Old Established Inn has to offer, will, he trusts, meet with and retain their approval and support.

Neat Post Chaise, and good Horses.—Funeral Equipages.

Lock-up Coach Offices, &c., &c.

HOLMES HALL,

ANCIENTLY THE SEAT OF

THE EARLS OF EFFINGHAM,

AND MOST DESIRABLY SITUATED NEAR THE STATION OF THE

NORTH MIDLAND RAILWAY,

AT MASBROUGH,

AND AT ITS JUNCTION WITH THE

SHEFFIELD AND ROTHERHAM RAILWAY.

A LICENCE having been obtained for the purpose of converting the above capital messuage with its extensive premises into an Inn, THE PROPRIETOR begs leave to call the attention of Families, Commercial Gentlemen, and other Travellers, on the above-mentioned lines of Railway, to the advantages connected with this Hall, &c., as an Inn, to those whom business or pleasure may call for a few days into this neighbourhood; combining, as it does, the pleasantness of a country residence, amidst the beautiful scenery surrounding Sheffield and Rotherham, with a close proximity to the extensive and rapidly increasing business marts connected with these places.

From this Inn (forming part of the projected New Town of Rotherham) the Traveller will reach Sheffield in quarter of an hour, Chesterfield in three quarters of an hour, Derby in one hour and three quarters, Station near Barnsley in three quarters of an hour; Station near Wakefield in one hour; and Leeds in one hour and a quarter, &c., &c.

NAC'S HEAD INN,

MARKET PLACE, ROTHERHAM.

J. FLINTHAM,

Master Gardener, Florist, and Seedsman,

Begs leave to return thanks to the Public generally, for favours already received in the above lines of business, and hopes by assiduity and attention to merit a continuance thereof

BEEF STEAKS AND CHOPS ON THE SHORTEST NOTICE.

Bentley's Entire, Best Beer, and Spirits of the best quality.

GOOD BEDS, &c.

BUTCHER'S ARMS,

CATTLE MARKET, CROFTS, ROTHERHAM.

G. DOBB

Begs leave to return thanks to Farmers, Butchers, Cattle Salesmen, and the Public, for favours already received, and hopes, by paying every attention to their accommodation, to merit a continuance thereof.

Market Breakfast table every Monday morning, extensive Stabling, Grazing for Cattle brought to market, and every accommodation for Farmers, Butchers and Salesmen attending the same

BLUE BELL INN,

MARKET PLACE, ROTHERHAM,

WILLIAM PERKINS,

Begs leave to return thanks to his Friends and the Public generally, for favours already conferred upon him, and to assure them that no attention on his part to their accommodation shall be spared to merit a continuance thereof

Fine Ales, Best Beer, and Spirits of the best quality.

Uni   ℞ ®

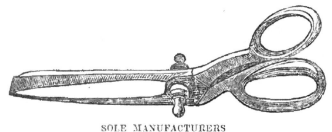

WILLIAM PARKER,

ATTERCLIFFE, NEAR SHEFFIELD,

SOHO WORKS,

AND

POND FORGE, SHEFFIELD,

MANUFACTURER OF

Spades and Shovels, all sorts
Shod-Tools
Grafting Tools
Paring Spades
Hay Spades
Cinder and Dust Shovels
Tulip Shovels
Stove Shovels, iron and wood handles
Stoaking Shovels
Crane Chains, all sizes
Chain Cables
Cart and Plough Traces
Rack Chains
Sacktackle Chain
Backbands
Cow and Beast Chains
Hames
Mill Chisels
Scrap Anvils
Vices, Scrap Iron
Oval and Round Frying Pans
Lead Ladles

Patten Rings
Spade Shafts
Waggon Clouts
Peal Plates
Water Tue Irons
Gavelocks
Scrapling Irons
Navigator's Picks
Stone Wedges
Sledge and Hand Hammers
Stone and Masons' Hammers
Blocks, all sizes
Tinmen's and Braziers' Tools, all sorts

STEEL.

Ⓛ Bar

Double Shear
Single Shear
Cast Steel
Coach Spring

Shear Steel made, Scrap Iron manufactured,

SPADES AND CAST TROWELS PLATED AT POND FORGE,

ROLLING AT THE SOHO AND POND FORGE MILLS.

TIMOTHY SCOTT,

PRINTER AND BOOKSELLER,

Removed from High-st.,

To larger Premises a little above the Cutler's Hall, in

CHURCH STREET,

SHEFFIELD.

THE

TEA WAREHOUSE,

ANGEL STREET,

Established for supplying the inhabitants of Sheffield and the public, with

TEAS

Of the choicest and most delicious flavours, at the lowest possible price,

BY

BALLANS AND COMPANY

Who beg to inform the public that their whole

TIME, TALENTS, AND CAPITAL,

are employed in the selecting of TEA. Their customers may at all times depend upon obtaining the best and choicest descriptions

OF

CONGOU, SOUCHONGS, NING YONGS,

SCENTED ORANGE PEKOES,

CAPERS,

FLOWERY, OR BLOSSOM PEKOES,

HYSONS,

YOUNG HYSONS, IMPERIALS,

AND

GUNPOWDERS,

AT A SMALL PROFIT ON THE FIRST COST PRICE.

TEA WAREHOUSE,

ANGEL STREET,   *SHEFFIELD.*

M. BARNES,
MANUFACTURER OF
SCISSOR KNIVES, PEN AND POCKET KNIVES,
TABLE KNIVES, &C.,
No. 13, ALLEN STREET, SHEFFIELD.

SHEFFIELD AND ROTHERHAM
CHEAP CLOTHING ESTABLISHMENTS.

THOMAS WILD,
45, FARGATE, 62, SNIG HILL,
(Opposite the Black Swan,)
SHEFFIELD,
ALSO TOP OF HIGH STREET, ROTHERHAM,

Begs most respectfully to inform his Friends and the Public that he has
always a large assortment of
New and Second-hand Clothes,
Consisting of Top Coats, Body Coats of all colours, Trowsers and Waistcoats,
of every description, also a large assortment of
WEST OF ENGLAND AND YORKSHIRE CLOTHS,
CASSIMERES, FANCY GOODS, WAISTCOATINGS, &c.,
In great variety.
Hats, Caps, Mackintoshes, &c., of the best manufacture.
N.B. MOURNING made to order on the shortest notice. The best Workmen
employed.

CHARLES F. YOUNG,
35, HIGH STREET, SHEFFIELD,
MANUFACTURER OF

SILVER AND SILVER PLATED GOODS,
JEWELLER, CUTLER,
AND GENERAL FURNISHING IRONMONGER.

This extensive Establishment and Suit of Rooms, offers to the inspection of the public,

A LARGE AND CHOICE SELECTION OF

FINE JEWELLERY,
Consisting of

LADIES' AND GENTLEMEN'S GOLD AND SILVER

ENGLISH AND FOREIGN WATCHES,
Of the best quality and workmanship,

GOLD, NECK, AND GUARD CHAINS,
EAR-RINGS, SUITS, &c., &c.,&c.,

SILVER, TEA AND COFFEE SETS, SPOONS, FORKS, &c.

AND ALL OTHER

ARTICLES IN SILVER PLATE.

PLATED TABLE SERVICES, VIZ:—

Dishes and Covers, Corner Dishes, Epergnes, &c., to correspond; LARGE and SMALL WAITERS, with rich Silver Mountings and Shields; Tea and Coffee Sets, ; Swing Kettles; Candlesticks and Branches, and all other articles; Table and Pocket CUTLERY in all its branches; Bronze and Or-Molu Table and Chimney Piece Ornaments; Spring Time Pieces; Cabinet Wares; Fancy articles in Silver, Mother-of-Pearl, and Tortoise Shell, &c., Papier Machee and Japanned Trays in extensive variety; Suspending and Table Lamps, &c., &c.; Bronze and Steel Mounted Fenders, Polished Fire Irons, and all other articles in the Furnishing Department.

Livery Dies and Buttons, Arms, Crests, and Mottos, &c., Engraved on Seals, Plate, &c., to order.

C. F. Y. will have much pleasure in showing his Establishment to Parties passing through Sheffield, as he trusts it will deserve their attention.

JOHN AND WILLIAM RAGG,
NURSERY, SHEFFIELD,
SOLE MANUFACTURERS
OF THE

NAPOLEON AND PARAGON RAZORS,
OF PRE-EMINENT EXCELLENCE;

ALSO,

SCISSORS
In every variety, from the lowest to the most elegant and costly.

ARTIFICIAL TEETH AND GOLD PALATES.

Mr. ESKELL, Surgeon Dentist.

The loss of Teeth supplied on the improved principle, whether arising from neglect, disease of the gums, or age; from a single Tooth to a complete set, without extracting the roots, or giving any pain, and in every case restoring perfect articulation and mastication. Mr. Eskell assuring the public, that he has brought the science to that state of perfection that the Artificial Teeth are not discernible from the productions of nature, and likewise warranted to bite the hardest substance without pain or inconvenience; tender and decayed Teeth effectually preserved from further decay, and every case appertaining to his profession submitted to his care, will meet with immediate attention,

AT HIS ESTABLISHMENT,

99, Norfolk Street, opposite St. Paul's Church,
SHEFFIELD.

SAMUEL COCKER AND SON,

PORTER WORKS, SHEFFIELD,

MANUFACTURERS OF THE

Best refined Steel Files, Wire Hackle and Gill Pins, Spiral Springs, Awl Blades, Wool Comb Brooches, Needle Pointed Card Cloth ;

AND

NEEDLES

MADE BY PATENT MACHINERY.

LONDON OYSTER ROOMS,

WATSON'S WALK, SHEFFIELD.

PAUL ASHLEY

BEGS to return thanks for the support with which he has been favoured, and to announce that his engagements in London enable him to have a *daily supply* of the

Best Native Oysters, direct from the Boats.

Those Friends who may favour him with their Orders, can have any quantity sent direct from Town, by informing him three days previous to the time required.

Out-doors ....1s. and 1s. 3d. per score.	Barrels ....6s. and 8s. each
In the Rooms..1s. 4d. ditto.	Double Barrels....16s. ditto.

Private Oyster Room up stairs.——Country Orders duly executed.

INDIA PALE ALE.

This favourite BEVERAGE, brewed expressly for the EAST INDIES, is strongly recommended by the Faculty in this Country, for persons suffering from Bilious Complaints, Indigestion, &c., and may be drank even by the most delicate, with whom no other Malt Liquor will agree.

From the extreme perfection to which this Ale has been brought, to enable it to withstand the effects of an Indian climate, it is divested of every particle of acidity, and is a most delightful Summer Beverage; and at the table of the Connoisseur, entirely supersedes Porter and other heady kinds of Malt Liquor.

To be had both Draught and in Bottle, of

P. ASHLEY,

25, London Oyster Rooms, and 26, Waterloo Wine and Spirit Vaults,

WATSON'S WALK, SHEFFIELD.

Pints....4s. per Dozen for Cash.——Quarts....7s. 6d. ditto, ditto.

Bottles and Hampers charged, and allowed for when returned.

Wines and Spirits.

BURTON AND HOME BREWED ALE.

LONDON BOTTLED AND DRAUGHT PORTER, ETC.

The *Sun* newspaper received daily; *Bell's Life in London*, the *York Herald*, *Sheffield Mercury*, and *Doncaster Gazette*, as soon as possible after publication.

N.B.—The rooms for the purveying of Oysters are open for Gentlemen to give orders; and the India Pale Ale may be had in draft at 2½d. per glass, or 10d. per Quart; or in Small Bottles at 4d., and Large Bottles at 8d.; as also the Strong Burton Ale, and home-brewed Beer.

HENRY HAWKSWORTH,

31, EARL STREET, SHEFFIELD,

MANUFACTURER OF

JOINER'S TOOLS, SKATES,

BRACES, BITS. GIMBLETS, &c., &c.,

Of every description and superior quality.

SPEAR AND JACKSON,

STEEL CONVERTERS AND REFINERS,

MANUFACTURERS OF

SAWS, FILES, EDGE TOOLS,

LEDGER BLADES,

CURRIER'S KNIVES, MACHINE KNIVES, &c.,

SAVILLE WORKS, SHEFFIELD.

T. WILEY,

Foreign and British

WINE AND SPIRIT MERCHANT,

AND

GENERAL NEWS AGENT,

Old Haymarket, (opposite the Tontine,)

AND

No. 2, CASTLE FOLDS,

Sheffield,

THANKFULLY acknowledges the liberal support he has hitherto received, and which his system of business has secured to him in Sheffield and neighbourhood, begs to inform the inhabitants of Rotherham and surrounding Villages, that he imports all his own goods, and pays the Queen's duties upon the same himself, which not only prevents the possibility of adulteration in quality, or deterioration in strength, but enables him (having a wholesale license) to serve families and others in small or large quantities, at "*Trade*" prices, viz.:—

	Gallon.	Quart.	Bottle.
	s. d.	s. d.	s. d.
Old French Brandy (the very best imported) ..	32 0	8 0	5 4
Betts's celebrated Brandy (full legal strength) ..	16 0	4 0	2 8
Very old Pale Jamaica Rum (best imported) ..	16 0	4 0	2 8
Curious White ditto ditto (overproof) ..	18 0	4 6	3 0
Nicholson's best quality unsweetened Gin..	12 0	3 0	2 0
Morayshire small-still Malt Whisky (overproof)..	21 0	5 3	3 6
Fine rich Cordials and Stomachic Bitters	12 0	3 0	2 0

Foreign Wines.

	Dozen.	Bottle.	Qrt.
	s. d.	s. d.	s. d.
Superior old full-flavoured Port	30 0	2 6	3 8
Very excellent Golden Sherry	30 0	2 6	3 8
Superior rich Tent Wine	32 0	2 8	4 0
... Cape Madeira	20 0	1 8	2 6
.... Cape Trinacia Dinner Wine	21 0	1 9	
.... Sicilian and Sardinian ditto	22 0	1 10	
Very superior old Pale and Golden Sherries ..	36 0	3 0	
.... Crusted Port	36 0	3 0	

British Wines.

Superior rich Raisin, Red and White Currant, Orange, Gooseberry, Ginger, Elder, &c... ..	16 0	1 4

The above Wines are in full-sized Wine Quarts—the Bottles charged 3s. doz. and allowed for if returned.

Guinness's celebrated Dublin Stout, Elliott's London mild and Brown Stout Porter, in quart and pint bottles, and Wiley's Amber Ale, in casks of all sizes.

N.B.—Orders by Post, Carriers, and Servants, strictly attended to in quality and measure; and, for facilitating business, a large quantity of Wines and Spirits are kept ready put up in all sized glass and stone bottles, sealed and labelled, and the carriage paid twenty miles round Sheffield.

JOHN NOWILL AND SON,

17, *MEADOW STREET, SHEFFIELD,*

Manufacturers of

SILVER FRUIT,

Silver and Silver Plated Dessert Knives,

And every description of

PEN, POCKET

SPORTSMAN'S, ERASING, AND DESK
KNIVES;

SUPERIOR RAZORS AND TABLE CUTLERY;

NAIL FILES;
BUTTON-HOOKS, STILETTOES, &c.;

Also articles for

LADIES' WORK BOXES

AND

Gentlemen's Dressing Cases,

In great variety.

J. N. and Son respectfully invite the attention of Merchants and the Public, to their long established and highly reputed Corporate mark, �✳ first granted by the Cutler's Company to Thomas Nowill, in the year 1700.

ATKINSON AND BRITTAIN,

(Bottom of Angel Street,)

Sheffield,

LINEN AND WOOLLEN DRAPERS,

SILK MERCERS, &c., &c.,

DEALERS IN CARPETS,

AND

LINCOLNSHIRE LIVE GOOSE FEATHERS;

A Large Assortment of Furs, Macintosh's Waterproof Coats, Caps, &c., &c.

WILLIAM NOWILL,

No. 126,

ROCKINGHAM STREET, SHEFFIELD,

(Late W. and J. Nowill,)

MANUFACTURER OF

SILVER FRUIT & DESSERT KNIVES,

AND EVERY VARIETY OF

PEN AND POCKET KNIVES, NAIL FILES,

BUTTON-HOOKS, STILETTOES, &c.

SUPERIOR TABLE CUTLERY.

DUKE'S PLACE,

50, ROCKINGHAM LANE, DIVISION STREET,

SHEFFIELD.

HENRY DUKE,

German Silver and Brass Founder,

MANUFACTURER OF

BRITISH PLATE,

WIRE, AND SNUFF BOXES.

ALSO OF

SCALES, SPRINGS, SHIELDS,

AND OTHER ARTICLES OF CUTLERY.

DOOR PLATES,

OF ANY KIND OF METAL, GOT UP IN THE FIRST STYLE
AND ON THE SHORTEST NOTICE.

H. DUKE flatters himself that, by long experience and the late improvements he has made by adding Steam Power to his Works, he will be able to serve his Friends and the Public with the above Articles, equal in quality and cheapness to any House in the Trade.

N.B.—STEAM POWER TO LET,

Connected with entire rooms, free from that inconvenience and dust which arises from Grinding Stones.

THORNCLIFFE

IRON WORKS,

NEAR

SHEFFIELD.

NEWTON, CHAMBERS, AND Co.,

MANUFACTURERS OF

PIG IRON,

PLAIN

AND

ORNAMENTAL CASTINGS,

OF

EVERY DESCRIPTION.

ANDREW BADGER,

LONG CROFT,

Sheffield,

MANUFACTURER

OF

BOOT HEEL PLATES

AND

STEEL PINS,

AND

Caster of Cutlery,

WHOLESALE AND FOR EXPORTATION.

NORTH STREET WORKS.

BROADHEAD AND ATKIN,

MANUFACTURERS OF

BRITANNIA METAL GOODS,

𝔖𝔥𝔢𝔣𝔣𝔦𝔢𝔩𝔡.

☞ THE ARTICLES PRODUCED IN THIS MANUFACTORY HAVE
GRADUALLY ADVANCED TO THE HIGHEST REPUTE:

THIS IS FULLY TESTIFIED BY THE INCREASING DEMAND FOR
THEIR

TEA AND COFFEE POTS,

COFFEE PERCOLATORS,

SPOONS, FORKS, LADLES, &c., &c.

B. and A. particularly invite attention to the recent improvements made in TEA and COFFEE POTS of their manufacture,
by the introduction of *their solely invented* non-conductors, by
which Britannia Metal Handles are entirely prevented from
becoming hot when in use; an improvement which was greatly
required.

T. WATSON, AND Co.,

No. 6, FARGATE,

Sheffield,

GROCERS, TEA DEALERS,

AND

CONFECTIONERS.

T. WATSON AND Co., beg leave most respectfully to inform the Gentry, Merchants, &c., of the Town and its Neighbourhood, that they supply all Articles of Confectionary required for Parties, &c., of the best description, and in the most elegant style.

A SUPPLY OF

FOREIGN PRESERVED

AND

DRIED FRUITS

Of the best Quality, constantly on hand.

ORANGES,

LEMONS, SAUCES, PICKLES,

&c., &c., &c.

CHARLES S. R. SANDFORD,

PHŒNIX FORGE

AND

IRON FOUNDRY,

MASBROUGH,

MANUFACTURER OF

"*DODDS' AND OWEN'S*"

PATENT

WROUGHT IRON RAILWAY WHEELS,

AND VARIOUS OTHER DESCRIPTIONS OF

CAST & WROUGHT IRON WHEELS,

HEAVY WROUGHT IRON WORK

FOR

MARINE AND OTHER ENGINES;

ALSO,

EVERY DESCRIPTION OF WROUGHT IRON WORK

FOR

RAILWAY CARRIAGES, &c.

SHIP HOTEL

NEAR THE RAILWAY STATION,

ROTHERHAM.

The above **Inn** having been entirely rebuilt and enlarged at an expense **of upwards** of £2,000, and being most desirably situated, within a minute's walk of the

RAILWAY STATION,

J. PARKIN,

Begs leave **most** respectfully to inform the public generally, that no expense **will be** spared in the furnishing and fitting-up of the house, in a **superior** manner, in order to ensure to Families, Commercial Gentlemen, and others, that accommodation and comfort, which he trusts will entitle him to their patronage and support.

J. P. cannot omit this opportunity of returning thanks to his Friends for **favours already** received, and hopes by assiduity and attention, to **merit** a continuance thereof.

WINES AND SPIRITS

Of the very best quality.

Excellent **Stabling,** Lock-up Coach Houses, Grazing for Cattle brought to **market,** and every accommodation for Farmers and Salesmen **attending** the same.

VICTORIA

PRINTING OFFICE,

HIGH STREET, ROTHERHAM.

JONATHAN BROWN,

Letter-press and Copper-plate

PRINTER,

BOOKSELLER, BOOKBINDER,

AND

MANUFACTURING STATIONER.

Posting and Hand Bills, Circulars, Lists of Prices, Catalogues, and every variety of Letter-press printing, executed with neatness, accuracy, and dispatch.

BOOKS BOUND IN EVERY VARIETY OF STYLE.

Ledger, Journal, and all other Account Books, ruled by machine on the premises, to any pattern, and bound on the improved principle *to open perfectly flat.*

Paper Hangings, comprising every variety, and suitable for every description of Rooms, &c.

JOSEPH HINCHLIFFE,

PRINTER, BOOKSELLER, BOOKBINDER,

AND

STATIONER,

Top of Westgate, Rotherham.

BIBLES, TESTAMENTS, AND BOOK OF COMMON
PRAYER,

WATTS' AND WESLEY'S HYMNS, &c.,

In plain and elegant Bindings,

Account Books ruled and bound to pattern on the premises.

☞ SCHOOLS SUPPLIED.

Depository for the Tract Society's Publications.

HENRY KIMPSTER,

MASBROUGH, ROTHERHAM,

MANUFACTURER OF

BOILERS FOR STEAM ENGINES,

ELL AND BACK BOILERS,

Gasometers, Gas Retorts,

WROUGHT IRON PANS OF ALL DESCRIPTIONS,

Scale Beams, Water Tue Irons, Hammers, Pickaxes, Screw Bolts,
Straw Knives, and Knives for Paper Mills, Mill Spindles, and all
sorts of Mill Work, Cart Axletrees, Wheel Hooping, and General
Job-smith.

Printed by James Drake, 52, New-street, Birmingham.

Left margin: Manufactured by Joseph Gillott, at his Works, 59, Newhall-street, and Graham-street, Birmingham.

Right margin: Sold by all Stationers, and other respectable dealers in Steel Pens throughout the Kingdom.

GEORGE RICHMOND COLLIS & CO.,

(Late Sir Eduard Thomason's Manufactory,)

CHURCH STREET, BIRMINGHAM,

MANUFACTURERS OF

Articles in the highest Classes of the Arts,

IN

GOLD, SILVER, PLATED, BRONZE, AND OR-MOLU.

IN this Establishment is manufactured GOLD and SILVER PLATE, including Racing Cups, Dinner and Tea Services of various Patterns, COMMUNION PLATE and PRESENTATION PLATE made to description given; or, if required, a variety of elegant designs furnished for approval; Silver-mounted Plated Wares of every denomination; Plated Cutlery upon Steel, Cut Glass, Or-Molu, Candelabra, and Lamps, Manufacturers of Medals in great variety, adapted for Societies and Institutions. Amongst the numerous series of Dies, are the celebrated Dassier Dies of the Kings of England, the Mudie Dies, for the series of grand National Medals, commemorative of the Victories of the late War; and forty-eight Dies, for Medals of the ELGIN MARBLES; also, SIR EDWARD THOMASON'S splendid series of one hundred and twenty large Medal Dies, illustrative of the HOLY SCRIPTURES, and a series of sixteen Medals upon Science and Philosophy, for Societies; Livery Button Dies cut, and the Buttons made; numerous patent Mechanical Inventions in the Metals, Pâpier Machee, Brass and Bronze Staircases, manufacturers of fine Gold Jewellery of the most splendid descriptions, dealers in Diamonds, Pearls, and fine Gems; Diamond Suits made to order, and altered to the present style, or, if required, purchased, and payment full value in cash; English and Foreign Money exchanged; Old Gold and Silver articles re worked as New, or Pur-chased.——Manufacturers of Sportsmen's Fine Fowling Pieces, upon an improved principle Duelling Pistols, Rifles, Air-Guns, and Canes, and Guns of every variety for exportation

Messrs. COLLIS and Co. inform the Nobility, Gentry, and their numerous Friends, that having very considerably enlarged their Works, are now enabled to manufacture the whole of their goods from the raw material to the finish. It will be evident that purchasers will find very considerable advantages in obtaining articles of very superior quality at such moderate prices that none but a Manufacturer could be enabled to supply. Their whole trade being with the consumers, Messrs. C. and Co. feel confident that all persons furnishing, or requiring their goods, will find it of undeniable advantage to pay them a visit, either personally or by letter, rather than make their purchases from shops that are only the retailers of goods made by the manufacturers, and necessarily sold at a very considerable advance of price.

These extensive SHOW ROOMS and MANUFACTORY are situate in Church Street, in the centre of the Town, adjoining St. Philip's Church-yard. The Ware-Rooms contain the Finished Articles for Sale, and are open to all persons of respectability.

The fac-simile of the celebrated WARWICK VASE, of upwards of twenty-one feet in circumference, was made in metallic Bronze at this Manufactory. The Copper Bronze Statue of His late Majesty, George the Fourth, upwards of six feet in height, was modelled, cast, and sculptured, at this Establishment, as also a Shield in honour of the Duke of Wellington's Victories. These and numerous other works are stationed in separate rooms to exhibit the progress of British Art.——Servants are appointed to conduct Visitors over the different Workshops, to whom and to the Work-people, the Visiter is requested to abstain from giving any gratuity

N.B.—Mr George Richmond Collis is Vice-Consul for France, Russia, Portugal, Turkey, &c, with the privilege of granting Passports to persons visiting France and its Dominions

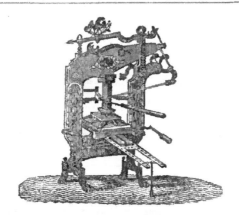

PRINTING OFFICE.

J. DRAKE, 52, NEW STREET, BIRMINGHAM,

Respectfully solicits the orders of his Friends and the Public in this department of his Business, which shall be executed with dispatch, and in a superior manner, at the prices affixed.

LETTER-PRESS PRINTING

EXECUTED IN THE NEATEST STYLE, AND WITH PLAIN OR FANCY LETTER ON GOOD PAPER AND CARDS.

	100.	200.	300.	400.	500.
Post 8vo. Circular, fly leaf ..	0 4 6	0 5 6	0 8 0	0 9 0	0 10 0
Ditto 4to. ditto ditto ..	0 7 6	0 8 6	0 11 0	0 12 0	0 13 0
Foolscap 8vo. Bill Head ..	0 4 0	0 4 6	0 6 0	0 6 6	0 7 0
Ditto 4to. ditto ditto ..	0 4 6	0 5 0	0 7 6	0 8 0	0 10 0
Ditto folio ditto ditto ..	0 5 0	0 7 6	0 10 6	0 13 0	0 15 0
Address Cards, common size ..	0 3 0	0 5 0	0 7 0	0 9 0	0 11 0
Ditto ditto, large ..	0 4 0	0 6 6	0 9 0	0 11 6	0 14 0
Ditto Third large ..	0 2 8	0 4 4	0 6 0	0 7 8	0 9 4
Handbills or Catalogues, Demy 4to.	0 8 0	0 9 6	0 12 6	0 14 0	0 15 6
Ditto ditto, Demy folio ..	0 15 6	0 17 0	1 1 6	1 4 0	1 6 6

☞ *Other sizes and descriptions of work at proportionate prices; and where a large number is ordered, the price is considerably less.*

N.B.—COPPER-PLATE AND LITHOGRAPHIC PRINTING ON REASONABLE TERMS.

☞ BOOKS and PAMPHLETS Printed at this Office, and Published in London and in all the Towns in the Midland District, upon advantageous terms.

WORKS

PRINTED AND PUBLISHED BY J. DRAKE,

52, NEW STREET, BIRMINGHAM,

AND SOLD BY HAYWARD AND MOORE, LONDON, AND ALL OTHER
BOOKSELLERS.

RAILWAY PUBLICATIONS.

Drake's Road Book of the entire Line of Railway from London to Liverpool
and Manchester—with Views and Maps. Price, foolscap 8vo , 4s. 6d.;
large paper, with engravings, &c.

Drake's Road Book of the London and Birmingham Railway—with a coloured
Map and Views. Price 2s., large paper, with steel engravings, 4s. 6d.

Drake's Road Book of the Grand Junction Railway—with a Map and Views.
Price, foolscap 8vo., 2s. 6d. ; large paper, with steel engravings, 5s

Drake's Road Book of the Nottingham and Derby, and Derby and Birmingham Railway. Price, foolscap 8vo., sewed, 1s. ; cloth, 1s. 6d.

Maps of the entire Line of Railroad, from London to Liverpool and Manchester—with the Time, Fare, and Distance Tables, &c. Price on Canvass,
in a case for the pocket, 2s.

Tables of the Times, Fares, and Regulations of the Grand Junction Railway.
—Published by authority. Including, also, the branch traffic, conveyance
by omnibuses, hackney coaches, and cars, and all other information requi-
site for travellers on this line. Price 3d. , or with a Map of the Line. 6d

Drake's Railway Sheet of the London and Birmingham, Grand Junction,
Aylesbury, Liverpool and Manchester, North Union, Newcastle and Carlisle, Newcastle and North Shields, Leeds and Selby, London and South
Western, Great Western, &c., Railways.—Price 4d., in a neat case for the
pocket ; on pasteboard, 6d

TOPOGRAPHICAL WORKS.

Drake's Picture of Birmingham—third edition, greatly improved; being a
concise but comprehensive historical and descriptive account of that place,
intended for the use both of residents and visiters, with a Map and twelve
Views of public buildings; and a complete, and the only correct list of
the principal manufacturers. Price 4s., bound in cloth.

Drake's Map of Birmingham—on a sheet of imperial drawing paper. Size of
Map, 23½ by 20 inches. With a Map of the Boundaries of the Borough,
price 3s. 6d. ; or coloured, to show the wards, price 5s. On canvass, in a
case, plain, 6s. 6d.; coloured, 7s. 6d. Sold in a neat frame, plain, 8s. 6d. ;
coloured, 9s. 6d.

The Birmingham Street Director,—with a Map. Price 1s. in a neat case for
the pocket.

The Visiter s Guide to Birmingham, Liverpool, and Manchester.—Price 1s.

MISCELLANEOUS NEW WORKS.

An Introductory Lecture on the Anatomy, Physiology, and Diseases of the Eye.—By Richard Middlemore, Surgeon to the Birmingham Eye Infirmary, &c. Demy 8vo. Price 2s.

A Practical Treatise on the Human Teeth,—showing the Causes of their Destruction, and the Means of their Preservation, by William Robertson. Demy 8vo., with plates. Price 7s. 6d. extra cloth.

The Law and Practice of Landlords and Tenants,—with the most approved modern Precedents. By R. Shipman, Esq., editor of "Jones' Attorney's Pocket Book," and author of the "Attorney's New Pocket Book." Demy 12mo. Price 17s., cloth.

A Stepping Stone to the Law of Real Property:—being an elementary Treatise on the Statute of Uses. By H. Smythies, Esq. Royal 12mo., price 7s., boards.

Municipal Corporation Guide.—By R. Shipman, Esq. Price 1s.

A Treatise on the Diseases of the Eye. By R. Middlemore, M.R.C.S., Surgeon to the Birmingham Eye Infirmary. Two thick volumes 8vo., price 35s. boards.

   ☞ This book has become of standard authority and reference, and is highly commended in all the medical reviews and periodicals in which it has been noticed.

Facts and Observations on Midwifery,—in seven sections, embracing some of the most important diseases incidental to females. By J. T. Ingleby, M.R.C.S.L., Senior Surgeon to the General Dispensary; Surgeon to the Magdalen Asylum, and Lecturer on Midwifery at the Royal School of Medicine, Birmingham. Demy 8vo., 9s.

A New Arithmetical Table Book, and Counting House Guide. Price 1s.

The Monitor's Guide, or the first four rules of arithmetic. Price 1s.

Drake's Tradesman's Remembrancer, suitable to any year. Foolscap folio, 3s. 6d., half bound.

Luckcock's (James) Hints on Practical Economy in the Management of Household Affairs. Sewed, 6d.

Luckcock's Family Book of Reference. Sewed, 1s.
—————— Memoirs, by T. Clark, Jun. Sewed, 6d.

Errors of the Social System Displayed.—By W. H. Smith. Sewed, price 1s.

A Treatise on the usefulness of Gorse as Winter Feed for Cattle. Price 6d., sewed.

Washing Books—for the use of Gentlemen, 6d.; Ladies, 6d.; and Families, 1s.

ACTS OF PARLIAMENT:—The Reform Act; The Highway Act; Charter of the Incorporation of Birmingham; Bread and Marriage Act.

BIRMINGHAM ALMANACS:—Drake's Birmingham Sheet Almanac,—on a sheet of royal paper, price 8d.——Drake's Pocket Almanac and Mercantile Diary, price 1s.; ditto in roan tuck, 3s. 6d.——Drake's Midland Almanac and Yearly Advertiser, price, sewed, 1s.——Drake's Railway Sheet Almanac, price 8d.

A Popular and Concise Treatise on the Treatment and Cure of Pulmonary Consumption.—By George Bodington, Surgeon. Demy 12mo.

INDEX TO THE ADVERTISEMENTS.

WHICH ARE HERE CLASSIFIED ACCORDING TO THE TRADES.

Uni

22 145

CPSIA information can be obtained
at www.ICGtesting.com
Printed in the USA
LVHW080118100922
728007LV00004B/214